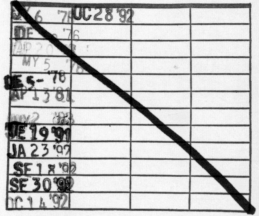

The Citizen in Court

The Citizen in Court

LITIGANT · WITNESS · JUROR · JUDGE

Delmar Karlen

DIRECTOR *The Institute of Judicial
Administration, New York University*

DRYDEN PRESS
HINSDALE, ILLINOIS

3 4 5 6 7 8 9   0 6 5   15 14 13 12 11 '10 9

Library of Congress Catalog Card Number: 64-18754
ISBN: 0-03-046130-8
Printed in the United States of America

Preface

The idea upon which this book is based is that law deserves a place in a liberal education. The reasons were suggested by de Tocqueville in his *Democracy in America* more than a century ago:

> Scarcely any political question arises in the United States that is not resolved, sooner or later, into a judicial question. Hence all parties are obliged to borrow, in their daily controversies, the ideas, and even the language, peculiar to judicial proceedings. As most public men are or have been legal practitioners, they introduce the customs and technicalities of their profession into the management of public affairs. The jury extends this habit to all classes. The language of the law thus becomes, in some measure, a vulgar tongue; the spirit of the law, which is produced in the schools and courts of justice, gradually penetrates beyond their walls into the bosom of society, where it descends to the lowest classes, so that at last the whole people contract the habits and the tastes of the judicial magistrate.

Laymen are not merely interested spectators of the judicial process, crowding into courtrooms, watching television accounts of trials, and reading mysteries, novels, and plays about the law. They are also participants, and to a far greater extent than in the work of the legislative or executive branches of government. Few indeed are the people who, never having been to court, can confidently expect that they will never have to go. Each year, traffic courts alone summon before them hundreds of thousands of citizens, most of them unaccompanied by lawyers. And who can be sure that he will never sue or be sued for a bill, or for a divorce, or for damages arising out of an accident?

Even if a man never becomes a litigant, his chances of involvement in the law are substantial. Something he has seen or heard may become the subject of judicial inquiry, and he may be called as a witness. Or he may sit on a jury to decide the fate of those accused of crime or the fortunes of those embroiled in civil controversy. He might even be elected a justice of the peace!

This book is designed to explain simply and briefly for the person who is not a lawyer what the courts are, and how they function. First, it sketches the structure of state and federal courts and their relationships to each other. Then it traces, step by step, a few common cases. A traffic offense, a robbery prosecution, a bill collection, a personal injury claim, and a divorce suit are analyzed with a view to showing how they are started, moved forward, and concluded. Here the roles of the parties, the witnesses, the lawyers, the jurors, the trial judge, and the appellate court are explained. Next comes a chapter on the interactions between the judicial branch of government and the legislative and executive branches. Finally, the book attempts to explain the process of decision-making—how judges and jurors decide whether witnesses are telling the truth, how they reason from circumstantial evidence, how they mold the law and apply it to the facts. At the end is a short annotated bibliography, suggesting further reading for those whose appetites have been whetted to learn more about law as a fascinating and pervasive influence in our society.

New York, New York

D.K.

May 1964

Contents

Preface   v

PART ONE   COURTS AND THEIR CASES

CHAPTER ONE   *The Machinery of Justice*   **3**

CHAPTER TWO   *A Traffic Offense (New Jersey)*   26

CHAPTER THREE   *A Robbery Prosecution (California)*   38

CHAPTER FOUR   *A Bill Collection (New York)*   58

CHAPTER FIVE   *A Personal Injury Case (Illinois federal court)*   46

CHAPTER SIX   *A Divorce Case (Nevada)*   80

CHAPTER SEVEN   *Appellate Review*   87

CHAPTER EIGHT   *Relations of the Judiciary to Other Branches of Government*   99

PART TWO THE PROCESS OF
DECISION-MAKING

CHAPTER NINE *Who Is Telling the Truth* 119

CHAPTER TEN *Circumstantial Evidence* 136

CHAPTER ELEVEN *Fitting the Law to the Facts* 155

CHAPTER TWELVE *Fitting the Facts to the Law* 180

Notes 195

Glossary of Terms 199

Bibliography 203

Index 207

The Citizen in Court

Courts

and
Their
Cases

Chapter / *One*

The Machinery
of Justice

The United States of America, unlike England and many other countries, has no single, unified system of courts. Instead, fifty-one systems are in operation, one for each of the fifty states and another for the federal government. The United States Constitution, which has established a central government of limited, enumerated powers, deals with judicial powers in the same manner as it deals with legislative and executive powers: It reserves to each state a very large measure of autonomy as to the number and nature of courts to be created and the manner of their operation.

State Court Structure

Since each state is free to create whatever courts it sees fit and to distribute judicial business among them as it sees fit, it is not surprising that great diversity exists between the judicial systems of the various states. Nevertheless, a general pattern can be discerned.

TRIAL COURTS At the bottom of the judicial hierarchy are the so-called inferior courts, which try minor civil cases (such as bill collections) involving small sums of money, and minor criminal cases (such as traffic offenses) involving light penalties. Inferior courts also conduct preliminary hearings in the more serious criminal cases, to determine whether the accused person should be released or held for trial in a higher court, but they do not in such hearings determine guilt or innocence or impose sentence.

Such courts are both numerous and highly localized, being found not only in every city, but in virtually every town, village, and hamlet in the land. Usually they are called *justice of the peace* courts, but in some places, particularly urban centers, they may go by other names, such as *municipal courts*. In metropolitan areas they are likely to be manned by full-time legally trained judges; but in rural areas the judges are often part-time officials and not infrequently laymen, without legal training.

Speaking of such courts in his home state, Chief Justice Vanderbilt of New Jersey said in words that are equally applicable elsewhere:

> It must be apparent to all who consider the matter that the local courts of first instance are the very foundation of the enforcement of the criminal law. On them rests the primary responsibility for the maintenance of peace in the various communities of the state, for safety on our streets and highways, and, most important of all, for the development of respect for law on the part of our citizenry, on which, in the last analysis, all of our democratic institutions depend. This is the underlying reason why I have repeatedly called the municipal courts the most important in our state. Not only is the work of the municipal court fundamental to the preservation of the social order, but . . . it comes in direct contact with thousands where the other trial courts only reach hundreds and where the appellate courts reach very few indeed. It is obvious that the use in the Constitution of New Jersey of the term "inferior courts" is a phrase, however it may be justified historically,

which should never be applied to the municipal courts. It is a court of first impression with limited jurisdiction, but it is in no respect an inferior court.[1]

Despite the wisdom of these observations, they have been little heeded. In far too many places, the minor courts are ignored by the legal profession and by the legislative bodies responsible for their existence. They are allowed to deteriorate to the point where they become inferior in fact as well as in position within the judicial hierarchy. Many justices of the peace are not only untrained in the law but elected to office because of considerations quite unrelated even to judicial temperament. Time devoted to their judicial duties is spared from farming, barbering, selling real estate, or otherwise earning a regular livelihood. They are poorly paid or, worse still, compensated by fees collected in the cases they try. They function all too often in dingy, shabby, even dirty surroundings— sometimes in courtrooms located in public buildings, but sometimes in their own homes, offices, stores, or filling stations. Their hours frequently are odd—Tuesday nights and Saturday afternoons, for example—or court sessions are scheduled irregularly only as business warrants.

Not all minor courts fit this description. Some—although relatively few—are courts of dignity manned by full-time professional judges, housed in suitable quarters, who conduct business at regular hours. These courts would more likely be found in metropolitan centers than in rural areas.

Regardless of the quality of a minor court and regardless of its location, the actual business that it handles is important. Especially is this true of those courts which, in addition to being entrusted with so large a share of responsibility for traffic safety, are also charged with handling other sensitive areas: juvenile delinquency, family support, and similar social problems.

Above the inferior courts are other trial courts, manned by full-time, legally trained judges. These courts handle the more serious cases—criminal trials carrying heavy penalties (like murder), and civil trials involving large sums of money (like actions for serious personal injuries).

Such courts are less numerous and less localized than the inferior courts and are usually organized on a county basis, one court to each county. If a county is in a metropolitan area, one or more judges is assigned permanently to that county. If it is a rural area, a single judge may serve several adjoining counties, traveling between them "on circuit." Hence the name *circuit court* frequently is used. Other names, however, are not unknown, among them *superior court, county court,* or *district court,* to mention but a few. The titles given judges also vary: A man sitting on the trial court of general jurisdiction in New Jersey is called a *judge* of the *superior court,* while his counterpart across the state line in New York is called a *justice* of the *supreme court.* (New York's terminology is exceptionally confusing.)

In some states, for instance California, such a court may possess truly general jurisdiction, for it is empowered to try all types of cases—civil, criminal, matrimonial, and probate. In other states, jurisdiction may be fragmented between several coordinate courts, one handling civil cases, another criminal cases, another matrimonial cases, another probate cases, and so forth. Colloquially, one of these coordinate courts (usually the one handling large civil cases) may be referred to as the *court of general jurisdiction,* but this is a misnomer. What is meant is only that its jurisdiction is broader than that of its sister courts, covering most, though not all, types of cases.

APPELLATE COURTS   In every state there is at least one appellate court, usually, though not invariably, called the *supreme court.* Again terminology varies widely from state to state. A man who sits on the highest court of New Jersey is called a *justice* of the *supreme court* of that state, while a man who holds an equivalent position in New York is called a *judge* of the *court of appeals.* Whatever the name of the court, it is the ultimate tribunal for hearing appeals from lower courts in the state, and so is often called the *court of last resort*. In a few cases, however, such of its decisions as involve federal questions are subject to further review in the United States Supreme Court, as we shall see in a subsequent chapter.

The judges who sit on appellate courts ordinarily do no trial work, being occupied exclusively in hearing appeals. They review the proceedings of trial courts upon the basis of written records. They hear oral arguments and read written arguments, called *briefs,* in an effort to discover whether errors were committed in the trial court of such a nature as to require reversal of the judgment or a new trial.

In the more populous states like California, Illinois, and New York, a set of intermediate appellate courts is sometimes interposed between the superior trial courts and the supreme court. Where the population is large and the litigation voluminous, and where there are many trial judges, the number of appeals tends to grow so large that it is not feasible to hear all of them in a single court. Hence two or more intermediate appellate courts may be established, each to hear appeals from the trial courts within a limited area of the state. Thus one court may hear appeals from the northern portion of the state, and another from the southern portion.

Legislative Sources of Decision

As a background for understanding the various kinds of cases handled in state and federal courts we must first look at the allocation of law-making power between the states and the central government.

Federal legislative power is limited to those areas entrusted to the central government by the Constitution of the United States. Congress is empowered, among other things, to regulate interstate and foreign commerce, establish post offices, declare war and maintain order, raise and maintain armed forces, punish counterfeiting and piracy, regulate naturalization, make rules on bankruptcy, patents, copyrights, and the like. In addition to its specific powers, Congress is authorized to make all laws "necessary and proper" for carrying into execution the powers vested in the central government. Within the areas enumerated, but only within them, Congress can impose criminal and civil responsibility upon individuals. It cannot define crime generally for the nation as a whole, nor can it establish a general national law of torts, contracts, or domestic relations. But when Congress acts within the sphere of its constitutional authority, it is supreme and its laws supersede any conflicting state laws.

All legislative power not vested in the central government is reserved to the several states, each of which is legally the equal of every other. No one of them is allowed to usurp the legitimate powers of any other any more than it is allowed to interfere with legitimate federal power.

The Common Law

Law is made not only by legislatures, but also by courts, as we shall see in detail in subsequent parts of this book. In fact, far more of the law currently in force in the United States comes from the courts than from legislatures. For this reason, a preview of the common law may be helpful at this point. That is the name given to the vast body of *precedents* created by judges in the course of deciding cases, and embodied, for the most part, in the written opinions of appellate courts. Today's judges feel obliged to follow precedents in deciding current cases, partly because they see no sense in working out a fresh solution for the same problem each time it recurs, and partly because they are convinced that one person ought to be treated as another person is, under similar circumstances. Without this conception, judges would be free to decide cases according to their private notions of right and wrong throughout the entire area of human relations not covered by statute. With it, the goal of stable and equal justice under law comes closer to realization.

The common law originated in England, and its fundamental ideas were brought to America by the early English settlers. There were few lawyers among them and few law books available, but the general principles of the common law were understood and, being familiar and generally acceptable, were applied by those who became judges (sometimes in a rather hit-or-miss fashion) to cases as they arose. In this manner, each colony "received" the common law and so filled a legal void that otherwise would have existed. In some places, the reception of the common law was formalized, as in this enactment of Maryland in 1639:

> Be it Enacted By the Lord Proprietarie of this Province of and with the advice and approbation of the ffreemen of the same that all the Inhabitants of this Province being Christians (Slaves excepted) Shall have and enjoy all such rights liberties immunities priviledges and free customs within this Province as any naturall born subject of England hath or ought to have or enjoy in the Realm of England by force or vertue of the common law or Statute law of England (saveing in such Cases as the same are or may be altered or changed by the Laws and ordinances of this Province).

Similar, though not identical, provisions are found in the laws of other colonies. For example, here is a later formulation of the same idea by Virginia in 1776:

> Be it ordained by the representatives of the people now met in General Convention, That the common law of England, all statutes or acts of Parliament made in aid of the common law prior to the fourth year of the reign of King James the first, and which are of a general nature, not local to that kingdom, together with the several acts of the General Assembly of this colony now in force, so far as the same may consist with the several ordinances, declarations, and resolutions of the General

Convention, shall be the rule of decision, and shall be considered as in full force, until the same shall be altered by the legislative power of this colony.

Such provisions recognized explicitly that the body of law thus received could be changed by legislation. Implicit in them was the further idea that the common law itself might change through judicial decision. The common law contained the seeds of further growth, for by its very nature it was an expanding, fluid, developing thing, reflecting each decision made.

It is not surprising that the common law developed differently in different areas. The judges of Pennsylvania, knowing little about decisions being made elsewhere and, in any event, not feeling bound by them, could hardly be expected to reach precisely the same results as the judges of Massachusetts, Delaware, or New York. As the nation moved westward and new states were formed in what hitherto had been wilderness, the common law moved westward too. In the Ordinance for the Northwest Territory, Congress in 1787 provided that judicial proceedings should be conducted "according to the course of the common law." By that time, of course, it had grown from what it had been a decade or certainly a century earlier. The changes had been gradual, so slow as to be scarcely perceptible, but they were real nevertheless. As new state constitutions were adopted, they often contained provisions that the "common law" (meaning what had developed to that point) should continue in force until modified or altered by legislation. So the common law spread throughout the nation, even into states like Louisiana, California, and Texas, which had started with legal principles and institutions derived from nations other than England. This was inevitable in view of the constant interaction between people from all parts of the Union as the result of freedom of travel and commerce across state borders.

The common law continued to grow in separate units, the judges of each state proceeding along their own lines.

They sometimes cited decisions from other states insofar as they knew about them, for those decisions were interesting and persuasive, and represented attempts by similar persons to solve similar problems; but the judges did not consider themselves bound by these precedents.

Today, as a result, there are substantial differences as well as substantial similarities between the common law of Massachusetts and that of Texas or Ohio. Indeed, the differences and similarities in the common law of the various states are as great as those in their statutory law. Subject only to restrictions imposed by the United States Constitution, each state prescribes its own law, civil as well as criminal, substantive as well as procedural, judge-made as well as statutory. Thus, conduct that is criminal in Kentucky may be socially acceptable in Minnesota; grounds for divorce in Nevada may differ vastly from those recognized in Vermont; and a prosecution that would have to be initiated by the indictment of a grand jury in Maine can be initiated in California by the accusation of a prosecuting attorney.

State Court Jurisdiction

We are now in a position to understand the kinds of cases handled by state courts. Primarily, state courts are engaged in enforcing their own laws in cases that ordinarily involve only local activities and local people.

CRIMINAL CASES The idea that state courts deal primarily with local problems is clear in the area of criminal law. Each state possesses power to define criminal conduct within its own borders and to provide appropriate punishment. It enforces its own criminal law, not that of any other state or of the federal government. Hence if a man commits murder in Pennsylvania, he can be tried only in the courts of that state. If he has fled from it to another part of the country, he must be brought back by extradition to Pennsylvania to stand trial.

There are, however, limitations imposed by the United States Constitution. No state can criminally punish conduct sanctioned by the Constitution as this document is interpreted by the Supreme Court of the United States. If any state attempted to punish a Negro for enrolling in the state university, for example, its action would be unconstitutional and would be struck down—by military force if necessary.

Just as there are substantive limitations, so also are there procedural limitations imposed by the Constitution. If, for example, a state should attempt to deny to a person accused of a crime the right to be represented by counsel, its action would be invalid and nugatory.

Another constitutional limitation is that a state may not interfere with any of its sister states. If Missouri attempted to punish as criminal conduct that occurred in Oregon, or if it attempted to send its officers into that state to arrest a man, it would be usurping power. Again its action would be struck down.

These limitations resulting from the Constitution of the United States are enforceable not only in the federal courts but also the state courts. They are binding upon state judges no less than upon federal judges, for a clause of the Constitution, known as the *supremacy clause,* specifically provides that:

> This Constitution, and the Laws of the United States which shall be made in Pursuance thereof; and all Treaties made, or which shall be made, under the Authority of the United States, shall be the supreme Law of the Land; and the Judges in every State shall be bound thereby, any Thing in the Constitution or Laws of any State to the Contrary notwithstanding.

If any state judge, through ignorance or willful disobedience, fails to give effect to valid federal law, his action is subject to reversal in the Supreme Court of the United States.

The Court has had the responsibility many times in the past of invalidating state criminal laws and state criminal procedures that violated the Constitution or valid federal laws enacted in pursuance of it.

CIVIL CASES   Just as a state has power to define crime within its own borders, so also it has power to create civil rights and liabilities within those borders. The same constitutional limitations apply: A state may not defy federal authority (as by closing its schools to Negroes or interfering with interstate commerce) or usurp the powers of its sister states (as by legislating with respect to persons or property outside of its own territory). Subject to these limitations, however, it is free to prescribe the rules of contracts, torts, domestic relations, property, succession, and the like that shall govern activities within its borders.

A civil action, unlike a criminal prosecution, can be brought in a state other than the one where the events giving rise to it took place. A claim arising in Wyoming and governed by Wyoming law does not have to be tried in a Wyoming court. It can just as well be brought in a court of North Carolina, and, indeed, it may have to be brought there if that is where the defendant lives. Ordinarily (though not invariably) a Wyoming summons must be served within its borders. It is not effective elsewhere, for to make it so would diminish the sovereignty of other states. In such a situation, then, North Carolina enforces the liability asserted, and it does so traditionally according to the substantive law of the place where the liability arose (Wyoming) but according to the procedural law of the forum (North Carolina). In this respect, it acts in much the same manner as a court of England acts when enforcing a civil liability arising in France and governed by the laws of that nation. Fundamentally the same principles of public international law apply.

Those principles, however, are reinforced by provisions of the United States Constitution. If Wyoming should attempt, except in special circumstances, to serve its summons in North Carolina, its action would violate the due process clause of the Constitution. If North Carolina should entertain the case but refuse to apply the law of Wyoming, its action might violate another constitutional clause, which states that:

> Full Faith and Credit shall be given in each State to the public Acts, Records, and judicial Proceedings of every other State.

State courts also deal with civil liabilities created by federal law. Civil rights and duties created by Congress within the sphere of the authority vested in it by the Constitution are not ordinarily restricted to enforcement in the federal courts. State courts have an equal power and duty with federal courts to enforce them. Again the supremacy clause of the Constitution controls, even to the point of superseding any conflicting state laws.

Despite the fact that state courts enforce civil liabilities created by the federal government and by other states, most of their cases are local. The typical state case is one in which a local resident is suing another local resident on a claim arising locally and governed by local law.

Federal Jurisdiction

Superimposed upon the fifty judicial systems of the fifty states is a network of federal courts. In view of the broad jurisdiction of state courts, and particularly their power and duty to enforce federal law, one may wonder why there is any need for a system of federal courts.

The need for at least one such court is apparent. Uniformity of decision throughout the nation on questions of federal law is essential. If, on such questions, each state supreme court could rule finally, the United States Constitution might mean one thing in New York and something quite different in California, and a federal statute might be interpreted one way in Michigan and another way in Ohio. To resolve such possible conflicts, the Constitution established the Supreme Court of the United States as the final arbiter on questions of federal law.

The lower federal courts were not established by the Constitution itself, which says only that such courts may be established by Congress. The First Congress took advantage of this provision to establish a system of federal trial courts. Successive Congresses have altered their number and character from time to time but have never abolished them, despite their power to do so.

But again the question arises: Why are such courts needed? Here there are several answers.

Federal trial courts are needed to enforce the federal criminal law, which, as we have learned, is not part of the business of the state courts. State courts might be given that responsibility but that has not happened, nor is it likely to happen. The idea of having the courts of one jurisdiction enforce the criminal laws of another runs counter to deep-seated habits of legal thought. The norm is to have each nation and state enforce its own criminal laws in its own courts.

There are comparatively few federal crimes. As indicated before, most ordinary crimes—murder, robbery, rape, and the like—are defined by state legislatures and prosecuted in state courts. Federal courts deal with such crimes only if committed on federal territories or reservations or against federal instrumentalities. For the most part, their concern is with offenses against the narcotics laws, postal laws, immigration laws, customs laws, and other statutes that can be enacted within the power of Congress. Because of Congress' power to regulate interstate commerce, however, the catalogue of federal crimes is broader than one might expect, extending even to such matters as interstate kidnapping (the Lindbergh law) and interstate prostitution (the Mann Act). Indeed, the federal criminal code runs to almost 2500 sections. Nevertheless, the fact remains that federal concern with crime is far less extensive than state concern, and this fact limits the area of criminal jurisdiction exercised by the United States courts. Broad federal criminal jurisdiction also is exercised by courts-martial, but these, being agencies within the armed forces and not traditional courts, are beyond the scope of this book.

With respect to federal laws imposing civil liabilities, no feeling exists that their enforcement should be restricted to the federal courts. Such laws are traditionally enforceable outside of the jurisdiction of their creation, both in the international sphere and the domestic sphere. English courts enforce civil liabilities arising under the laws of France, and the courts of Massachusetts enforce civil liabilities arising under the laws of Illinois. And, as we have seen, state courts not only may, but must, enforce civil liabilities created by the federal government.

Nevertheless, despite the unquestioned capacity of state courts to enforce federal civil laws, federal courts are thought to be needed for civil as well as criminal cases. In some areas of federal law—including those pertaining to admiralty, bankruptcy, patents, and copyrights—federal courts are given exclusive jurisdiction. In other areas, they have jurisdiction concurrent with that of the state courts.

Why should there be two sets of courts, each duplicating the work of the other? An easy way to answer that question would be to reverse it, and ask: Why not? A given amount of judicial business requires the services of a given number of judges. What difference does it make that some of them may be employed by the federal government while others are employed by the state governments? This, however, is not a satisfying answer, for it seems to suggest that the vesting of civil jurisdiction in the lower federal courts is casual, even quixotic.

A better reason may be found in the need for relieving the Supreme Court of the United States of some of its burdens. The time and energy of that court is limited; it cannot review every decision of every state court on every federal question. If, therefore, some of those questions can be channeled into lower federal courts, there to be decided by judges who specialize in federal law and who can be expected to be sympathetic to its objectives, the pressure on the Supreme Court may be relieved. The lower federal courts' decisions will more likely be correct and more likely require no further review than decisions by state judges who cannot specialize in federal law and who may be unsympathetic to its purposes.

Whether this is an historically accurate reason for giving the lower federal courts jurisdiction over civil cases presenting federal questions or not, it will do as a current rationalization for the continuance of that jurisdiction. It explains why any plaintiff having a substantial claim based upon federal law may bring it into a federal court, and why any defendant against whom such a claim is asserted in a state court can remove it therefrom to a federal court.

Not every claim founded upon federal law is allowed to come into a federal court. In some types of cases the claim must involve $10,000 or more (if the claim is less substantial, even though based upon federal law, it must be prosecuted in a state court). Congress, in this manner, has attempted to limit the size of the federal judicial establishment and to restrict even the lower federal courts to important cases.

A final reason for having lower federal courts try civil cases lies in the fear that state courts may reflect local prejudice against nonresidents. In a nation where people move about as freely as they do in the United States, and where there is free and extensive commercial intercourse across state lines, controversies inevitably arise between the citizens of different states. Thus, a resident of Indiana, driving his automobile in Mississippi, may have a collision with a resident of that state. If he brings an action in Mississippi (which is probably the only place where a summons can be served), and if he goes into a state court there, he will be an outsider engaged in a contest with an insider; the case will be tried by a Mississippi jury before a Mississippi judge under Mississippi law. In such circumstances, the outsider may suffer because of local prejudice, or at least feel that he is the target of such prejudice.

Hence if his claim is for $10,000 or more, he is allowed to bring it into a federal court in the state of Mississippi. The substantive law to be applied will still be that of Mississippi. The jurors will still come from that state, and the judge will still be a resident of it, probably born and raised there. They will, however, be sitting in a federal courthouse. On the assumption that that fact makes a difference is predicated federal jurisdiction over diversity of citizenship cases. (A corporation, incidentally, is treated as a "citizen" of the state in which it is incorporated or has its principal place of business.)

Diversity cases involve no element of federal substantive law. The only federal law used is procedural, regulating the mechanics of litigation but presumably not affecting its outcome.

Even if judge-made rather than statutory law is involved, it is the judge-made law of the state that prevails. Federal judges must respect and apply it, just as they must respect and apply state statutes.

Until recently this was not so. Federal judges were free to introduce their own ideas of the common law in deciding diversity of citizenship cases. During the nineteenth century judges were less conscious than we are today that they make law in the course of deciding cases; they tended to regard the common law as a pre-existing body of rules covering all situations that might arise. The job of a judge, in this conception, was merely to discover the relevant principle and apply it to the case at hand. If he discovered it differently than another judge, that was unfortunate—one of the two must be mistaken—but neither could shirk the duty of applying the law as he understood it. Federal judges were no different in this respect than state judges. While the former would respect and apply state statutes in cases not governed by federal law, they balked at according equal respect to the judge-made law of the state. The common law was thought to be, in the colorful phrase of Supreme Court Justice Oliver Wendell Holmes, Jr., "a brooding omnipresence in the sky" rather than the sum total of the rulings of past and present judges, deriving their force from the power of the state which enforced them. This idea was productive of much mischief. Instead of unifying the law throughout the nation, it introduced new elements of uncertainty and complexity. A case that might be brought in a state court and there be decided one way might also be brought in a federal court where an opposite result could be reached. The outcome would depend not so much upon the facts of the case as upon the forum in which it was tried.

In 1938, the Supreme Court of the United States, in the landmark decision of *Erie Railroad v. Tompkins,*[2] decided that the old practice should be stopped and that henceforth there should be no general federal common law. The reason was constitutional: The federal government was one of limited, enumerated powers, not to be overstepped by its judicial branch any more than by its legislative branch. Just as Congress was prohibited from enacting statutes outside of the areas assigned to the federal government by the Constitution, so also the federal courts were prohibited from making law outside those areas in the course of reaching judicial decisions. Since 1938, they have been obliged to apply state common-law decisions to the same extent as they apply state statutes.

Removal of Cases

If a plaintiff chooses to bring a diversity of citizenship case in a federal court, the defendant cannot remove it to a state court. Removal is permitted only in the opposite direction—from state court to federal court.

If the plaintiff chooses instead to bring his action in a

court of the state where the defendant resides, again there can be no removal. The privilege of removal is accorded only to the defendant, never to the plaintiff, and only under certain circumstances. If the defendant is in a state court in his own home territory, there is no reason for him to fear local prejudice and so seek the protection of federal jurisdiction. If, on the other hand, the case had been brought in a court of the state where the plaintiff resided, the defendant could remove it to a federal court in that locality, but this seldom happens. Therefore, the plaintiff's choice between a state and a federal court for a diversity of citizenship case is ordinarily irrevocable. (The same is not true with respect to a federal question case, for if such a case is brought in a state court when it could have been brought in a federal court, the defendant has an absolute right to remove it to the federal court.)

The requirement that a diversity of citizenship case must involve $10,000 or more cannot be justified purely in terms of logic, for small cases as well as large ones may involve local prejudice. Like the similar requirement applying to some (though not all) federal question cases, it can be justified only in terms of the desirability of limiting the business of the federal courts.

Some observers believe that there is little justification today for federal jurisdiction over diversity of citizenship cases. While not denying that prejudice in litigation sometimes exists—against corporations in favor of individuals and against rich people in favor of poor people—these observers doubt that it takes the form of local prejudice against non-residents, or if it does, that it is any less severe in federal courts than state courts. This point of view may ultimately prevail for it is now the subject of serious official and scholarly reconsideration. Nevertheless, at the present time, jurisdiction over diversity of citizenship cases is one of the two great sources of the civil business of federal courts, the other being jurisdiction over federal question cases.

Federal Court Structure

The structure of the federal judicial system is similar to what is found in the various states. There are three levels of courts: trial, intermediate appellate, and top appellate.

DISTRICT COURTS The trial courts are called *district courts*. There are ninety-one such, one for each of the judicial districts into which the nation is divided. In areas of relatively light population, district boundaries are likely to be coterminous with state boundaries, for every state has at least one United States district court. In areas of heavy population they are likely to embrace only a portion of a state. Thus in New York there are four districts whereas in Maine there is only one.

Whether a district court is manned by a single judge or by several depends upon the population of the district. The court for the Southern District of New York, which serves New York City and a few adjacent counties (the busiest in the nation) has twenty-four judges. Other districts have but a single judge.

The district court is on the same level as a state trial court of general jurisdiction, neither superior nor inferior to it. No appeal lies from either to the other, for both are courts of original rather than appellate jurisdiction.

The jurisdiction of the district courts is not as broad as that of many state trial courts. In general, it is limited to the three classes of cases already mentioned: prosecutions for federal crimes, civil claims based upon federal law, and civil claims between citizens of different states. With respect to criminal prosecutions and a small group of civil actions, the jurisdiction of the district courts is exclusive. With respect to the great majority of civil actions, it is concurrent with that of state courts. In situations where concurrent jurisdiction exists, a case tried in a state court must be appealed through the state judicial system, and a case tried in a federal district court must be appealed through the federal appellate system.

COURTS OF APPEALS There are eleven intermediate appellate courts, called *United States courts of appeals,* one for each of the circuits into which the nation is divided. There is one circuit for the District of Columbia alone (because of the need for judicial review of the great volume of federal administrative action taking place in the national capital), but each of the other circuits embraces several states. In an attempt to equalize, so far as feasible, the business of the various courts of appeal, Congress has created circuits of different sizes. Those along the eastern seaboard, where the population is heavy, embrace only a few states, whereas those in the western part of the nation cover many states. Thus the Court of Appeals for the Second Circuit hears appeals from federal district courts in three states: New York, Connecticut, and Vermont, while the Court of Appeals for the Ninth Circuit hears appeals from federal district courts in nine states: Washington, Oregon, California, Montana, Idaho, Nevada, Arizona, Alaska, and Hawaii.

The jurisdiction of each court of appeals is exactly the same as that of any other, the only difference between them being in the geographical origin of their cases. There is no differentiation between them as to subject matter. All handle criminal appeals as well as civil appeals.

Appeals to these courts lie only from the lower federal courts and from federal administrative agencies. They possess no power to review the decisions of state courts.

THE SUPREME COURT Decisions of the courts of appeals are subject to further review in the Supreme Court of the United States. A few go there as a matter of right, but most only as a matter of discretion exercised by that court. Whether discretionary or not, few cases go up—less than 5 percent on the average.

The Supreme Court is not only the highest federal

court, but also has power to review decisions of the highest courts of the various states insofar as they rest upon determinations of federal questions. It is thus the ultimate arbiter of federal law and the tying force that binds together all the courts of the nation. We shall consider it in greater detail in a later chapter.

Relative Roles of State and Federal Courts

There is a popular tendency to overestimate the importance of the federal courts. This is unfortunate, because the state courts form the backbone of the judicial system of the United States. They can handle substantially any case that the federal courts can handle as well as a great many more that the federal courts cannot touch. Those involving less than $10,000, for example, ordinarily cannot be brought in the federal courts. This is true even of some cases that involve federal questions. As for the great bulk of cases based upon state law and involving residents of the same state, these can be brought only in state courts, no matter how much money is involved. Most cases are of this nature: A resident of Illinois sues another resident of Illinois on a contract or tort arising in Illinois governed by Illinois law.

Most of the jurisdiction of the federal courts is concurrent with that of the state courts. While there are some cases over which the federal courts have exclusive jurisdiction, notably prosecutions for federal crimes, claims against the United States, and proceedings to review decisions by federal administrative tribunals, these do not bulk large in the total litigation of the nation.

As against about 400 judges in the federal courts, there are almost eight times that number in New York State alone, including justices of the peace. Excluding them, there are still almost twice as many judges in the courts of New York as in the entire federal system. A vastly greater number of civil and criminal cases are disposed of each year in the

New York State courts than in the entire federal system. It costs more money to run the courts of New York than it does to run the federal courts; and the New York judges are paid higher salaries than their federal counterparts—$34,500 per year for a judge of the supreme court of New York sitting in New York City, as against $22,500 for his colleague across the street sitting in the federal district court.

In terms of relative position, the federal district courts are on a par with state courts of general jurisdiction, and the federal courts of appeal are on the same level as state appellate courts. Only the Supreme Court of the United States has the power to review what the state courts decide and then only involving matters of federal law. On matters of state law state supreme courts have the last word.

The fact is that if the federal courts were to be abolished tomorrow, as could be done by Congress alone (without a constitutional amendment) so far as the lower federal courts are concerned, no overwhelming inconvenience would result. The specialized cases over which the federal courts have exclusive jurisdiction would have no place to go, but the great bulk of their cases could be taken over by the state courts, with no amendments necessary to expand their jurisdiction. There would be strain, of course, because the state courts are already overloaded with work, but the additional business could be handled by the addition of a relatively small number of new judges.

On the other hand, if tomorrow the state courts should be abolished, leaving only the federal courts, chaos would result. The load of new cases would be crushing, requiring a vast multiplication in the number of federal judges. Furthermore a constitutional amendment would be needed, for the present jurisdiction of the federal courts would not be broad enough to absorb the load. Only the few cases involving diversity of citizenship or federal questions could come in. The great bulk of cases—involving one resident of a state suing another resident of the same state on a claim arising in that state under the laws of that state—would not be within the federal judicial power as presently defined in the United States Constitution.

Despite the prestige of the federal courts and their unquestioned great importance, they are specialized tribunals occupying a relatively small place in the total court system of the United States.

Chapter / *Two*

A Traffic
Offense

The simplest as well as the most common type of case is a
prosecution for a minor offense. Yet, thoughtfully considered,
it can yield much information about the American legal
system, the distinction between civil and criminal cases, the
organization of courts, and the sources, nature, and purpose
of law.

Let us consider the routine case of a traffic offense,
which is committed many times every day over the entire
nation. Suppose that Martin Miller, whose legal residence is
in New Jersey but who works in Pennsylvania, is driving his
automobile on a highway in a rural county of New Jersey.
The speed limit is fifty miles an hour, but Miller is going
fifty-three. A state trooper in an official car passes him. Nothing happens. When, absent-mindedly, Miller lets his speed
drift up to fifty-nine miles an hour, another state trooper, approaching from the rear, sounds his siren, orders Miller to
pull over to the side of the road, and gives him a ticket. A
different officer might only have warned him to drive more
slowly.

The fact underscored by this incident is that law in
action is sometimes different from law in the books. Law is

not self-executing but works through human agencies. If the police officers of a given area customarily give speeding tickets only to motorists going ten or more miles above the posted limit, the effective speed limit in that area is sixty miles an hour, not fifty as stated in the statute. If, on the other hand, there is no such custom, then the effective law is, within limits, determined by the individual judgment of the police officer who happens to be on hand. He is not authorized to arrest a motorist who is going less than fifty miles an hour, but neither is he effectively obliged to arrest one who is going above that speed. He may have a personal idea that fifty-five miles an hour is the dividing line between speeding and proceeding properly.

Not all violations of law are prosecuted, not even all that are observed by law-enforcement officers. It would be a mistake, therefore, to assume that law operates with complete impersonality, or that such discretion as exists in its application is exercised only by judges, jurors, or district attorneys. They ordinarily never get a chance to exercise discretion in a criminal case until after some police officer has made a preliminary judgment that an offense has been committed which is worthy of prosecution. The goddess of Justice is not as blind as customarily represented, or as remote.

The Traffic Ticket

The ticket Miller receives is the nonfixable type, used in New Jersey and some other states. It is so called because each ticket is prenumbered and made out in quadruplicate. One goes to the motorist, another is retained by the officer, another goes to the state motor vehicle authority (for possible use in suspending or revoking drivers' licenses), and the final copy goes to court. Since each ticket must be accounted for, no single police officer or other official can conveniently forget about its existence once it has been issued. Even knowing the judge will not help, for he too is subject to accountability.

The ticket has two purposes. First, it serves as a written accusation that the defendant has committed a certain offense—a function that in serious criminal cases is performed by a more elaborate document called an *indictment* or an *information,* described in the next chapter. Second, it prescribes the time and place for the appearance of the defendant in court. He is not arrested and taken into custody as he would be if accused of a more serious crime (driving while drunk, for example). For most traffic and other minor offenses, a mere summons to appear is considered enough for local residents. Should the invitation be disregarded, a warrant for arrest may be issued and the accused taken to court in custody.

A nonresident, on the other hand, is likely to be taken into custody for speeding or a similar offense and brought forthwith to court. If he is merely given a ticket, it is difficult and cumbersome at best to enforce his court appearance, for to do so would entail the suspension by the motor vehicle bureau of his privilege of driving on the local highways, the communication of that fact to the man's home state, and the suspension by it of his home license until he makes peace with the state where his offense occurred. All this takes time and effort and involves much correspondence as well as cooperative effort between the two states involved. Nevertheless, sometimes it is impracticable to do anything but give the offending motorist a ticket, as for example when he is arrested on a super highway and the police officer cannot leave his post long enough to go to court. When that happens the motorist may or may not comply with the summons; and if he fails to do so he may or may not get into trouble, depending upon how willing his own motor vehicle bureau is to cooperate in the enforcement of the traffic laws of other states.

Choice of Court

The court to which Miller has been summoned is a municipal court in the county and state where he was apprehended. Why that court? Why not a federal court? Why not a court in Pennsylvania? Why not a different court in New Jersey?

These questions are more difficult than they seem. An attempt has been made to answer them more or less abstractly in Chapter One, but a brief summary is in order here, applied to the facts of this case.

The reason that a federal court would not be appropriate for Miller's case is that such courts lack power to enforce any criminal laws except those which emanate from Congress. Local traffic laws are beyond the power of Congress to enact, for the federal government is one of limited powers. The enumerated powers, while extensive, are nevertheless narrow when viewed against the totality of governmental activity. All powers not granted to the federal government are reserved to the states, and these include the power generally to define the legal relations between man and man, to establish their rights and duties, and to draw the line that separates proper conduct from that conduct which is regarded as criminal.

As for the courts of other states, including those in Pennsylvania where Miller works, they are as powerless to act as federal courts, and for much the same reason. They can enforce only the criminal laws of their own states, which are powerless to legislate with respect to activities outside of their own boundaries. Pennsylvania has no right to say what shall be the speed limit in New Jersey, and New Jersey has no right to say what shall be the speed limit in Pennsylvania. Each state is relatively sovereign within its own borders, free from interference by sister states.

Logically it might be possible for a court in one state to enforce the penal laws of another, just as it enforces civil liability created by that state. If a contract made in state A can be enforced in state B (as it can), then it would seem that a crime committed in state A should also be subject to prosecution in state B. Nevertheless, the course of history has been otherwise, perhaps in part for the practical reason that witnesses to a crime—often police officers—cannot feasibly be transported elsewhere to testify. Whatever the reason, the enforcement of criminal law is a localized affair. If a man is charged with having committed a crime in New Jersey, he can be prosecuted for it only in that state.

Even within the federal system, criminal law enforcement is localized. If a man commits a federal crime—for example, robbing a post office—he must be tried in the district where the crime took place. If apprehended elsewhere, he is brought back to "the scene of the crime" (in a legal sense, rather than in the sense of mystery fiction). This is required by the United States Constitution, and the requirement was inserted by the framers of that document for the benefit of accused persons in order to prevent a repetition of the colonial practice of transporting prisoners to England to answer for crimes allegedly committed in the colonies, thus depriving them of the testimony of local witnesses as well as forcing them to stand trial alone and away from home.

State constitutional and statutory provisions are to the same effect. They require not merely that a man be tried in the state where he is alleged to have committed his offense, but also in the county (or similar local subdivision) where it was committed.

We have still to consider why a municipal court is the appropriate one for Miller's case. The answer is twofold: first, it is a trial court, rather than one that hears appeals, and second, it is the court to which the legislature of New Jersey has entrusted the handling of this type of case. Here it is called a *municipal court* but in another state it might be called a *justice of the peace court* or *district court*. Technically, such a court ordinarily does not have exclusive jurisdiction over the cases assigned to it, for they can also be brought in courts of more general jurisdiction; but they seldom are, because of the cost, delay, and more cumbersome procedure involved. Hence a practical understanding springs up among the judges, lawyers, and law-enforcement officers of a community and reinforces the intention of the legislature that small cases will in fact go to the inferior courts.

Defendant's Appearance in Court

Now, having managed to get Miller into the proper court, we are faced with the question of why he is there. If the only purpose is to collect a modest fine, it could just as well be sent by mail and Miller spared the trouble and expense of going to court.

The purpose is not so limited, however; revenue from fines is but a by-product of the enforcement of the criminal law. The main purpose is quite different. An earlier generation would have said that it was to punish the offender. Today we are likely to say that the purpose is to reform him or to deter others from following his example (or in very serious cases to incapacitate him by death or imprisonment from doing further harm). By *reform* is meant not moral rejuvenation, but, more modestly, an experience from which the man learns that he has done wrong in a particular situation. The ideal is that he should gain an understanding of the purpose of the law he has violated. If, in a traffic case, he comes to realize that speed limits are imposed for the safety of himself and others, and that violations lead not only to unpleasant court appearances and fines, but, more important, to accidents and even to the loss of life, a major purpose of the criminal law has been achieved.

The offender is more likely to learn his lesson if it is accompanied not only by a fine but also by trouble and inconvenience, and perhaps also by extra expense in the form of lost wages. If he had merely to drop a check in the mail, he might quickly forget the incident and regard the fine as not more than a fee paid for the privilege of speeding. The effect upon others would also be lost, for they could reasonably anticipate similar treatment for similar conduct. If they feared nothing worse than the prospect of having to pay a fine, the deterrent effect upon them of Miller's case would be insignificant.

Despite these observations, most traffic courts have

violations bureaus in which clerks accept payments of fixed fines for specified offenses, especially minor ones. Sometimes the fines may even be sent in by mail. We shall assume that this procedure is not applicable in the present case.

A Plea of Guilty

The proceeding in court, so far as it directly concerns Miller, will probably last only a minute or two. He may have to wait some time while other cases are being heard, especially if the court is a busy one in a metropolitan area. Once his case starts it will move fast. His name will be called, he will step up in front of the judge's bench, the judge will read or state the substance of the charge and ask Miller how he pleads, guilty or not guilty. Miller will probably respond "guilty," and the judge will impose whatever fine he thinks proper. As Miller is handing the money to the judge (or to a clerk if one is present in this minor court), the judge will continue with the next case. The judge may add a few words to Miller on the importance of obeying traffic regulations or he may deliver a short lecture to him and the group of other traffic offenders at the beginning or end of the court session. It is also possible that Miller, at the time of his pleading guilty, may offer a few words of explanation or contrition. Even so, the whole proceeding is likely to be over in a very short time.

This, rather than the dramatic spectacle sometimes seen on television, is the typical criminal case.

Small Number of Contests

It is noteworthy that very few minor criminal cases are contested. Precise figures on the number of contests vary from one state to another and from one court to another even within a given state, but the general pattern is unmistakable—about 90 per cent of all defendants plead guilty.

The consequence is that there is no trial in the typical criminal case—only *arraignment* (the name given to the procedure whereby the defendant is informed of the charge against him and asked how he pleads) and sentencing. In most European countries this would not be true, for there, even if the defendant were willing to admit to the offense charged, an inquiry into the facts would still be required in order to determine guilt or innocence. Presumably this system is based on the theory that an individual is not necessarily capable of judging his own guilt or innocence. The government, it is believed, has a responsibility to see that the individual is not unjustly punished, for his liberty and property are community as well as personal assets and should be subject to forfeiture only after due, official inquiry.

In the United States, the practice is otherwise. Right or wrong, our assumption is that a man accused of crime knows whether he is guilty or not. If he admits guilt, we operate on the assumption that a trial would be a meaningless, expensive, and time-consuming ritual, and we dispense with it.

A Plea of Not Guilty

If the defendant wants a trial, he may have it. All he has to do is plead not guilty, and trial will take place either forthwith or after an interval during which the judge disposes of other cases not requiring trial. In a metropolitan court, the case might have to be adjourned to another day, thus adding to the trouble and inconvenience.

The trial probably will be short and simple, lasting no more than five or ten minutes. No jury will be present, for the constitutional right to trial by jury in most states covers only serious charges. Sometimes this is by virtue of an express constitutional or statutory provision, sometimes by virtue of judicial interpretation of a seemingly broad guarantee of trial by jury for all criminal prosecutions. Despite such sweeping language, the standard (though not universal) interpretation is that this mode of trial is available today only in the same type of prosecutions as were triable by jury at common law in England. The prevailing theory is that the right was intended only to be preserved by the constitutional guarantees, not extended. Since in England petty offenses were triable summarily by magistrates sitting without juries, the same type of offenses can be tried today without juries in the United States.

Nor, in all probability, will any lawyers be present at the trial. The defendant is entitled to have a lawyer, but he would probably regard the expense as unjustified, for the problem seems too simple to require specialized knowledge. In serious criminal prosecutions and in civil actions involving substantial sums of money or important property rights, lawyers are usually considered necessary. Not so in traffic cases, even when they result in trial.

On the prosecution side, much the same feeling about using lawyers prevails. The county attorney could—perhaps should—be present, but he seldom is. Often he is a part-time official engaged in the private practice of law as the chief source of his livelihood, and he has little time to devote to minor cases that can be handled by police officers. The burden of prosecution, therefore, falls upon them, with the result that in the type of case we are now considering lawyers are conspicuous by their absence. All the leading roles in the trial are likely to be played by laymen—judge, prosecutor, and defendant, acting as his own counsel.

Once the defendant has been arraigned and has pleaded not guilty, the evidence is presented. It usually consists, on the prosecution's side, only of testimony by the arresting officer. After being sworn to tell "the truth, the whole truth, and nothing but the truth," he takes the witness stand (if there is one in the courtroom; otherwise he stands in front of the judge) and relates his version of what happened.

Usually his story is brief and can be told in a few sentences, supplemented by answers to whatever questions may be put to him by the defendant as cross-examination or by the judge.

Then, since there are rarely any other witnesses, it is the defendant's turn. He need not testify, for he has the constitutional right to remain silent. This is known as the *privilege against self-incrimination*. Important as this privilege may be in other circumstances it is largely theoretical in the situation in which the defendant finds himself in a traffic case. There is little point in his pleading not guilty and having a trial if he does not wish to testify, for the likelihood of a collapse of the prosecution's evidence on issues as straight-forward as those involved in a traffic case is very slight. Assuming, then, that he decides to testify, he does so under oath, giving his version of what happened. Like the police officer, he is subject to cross-examination by the opposing side and questioning by the judge.

Judgment or Decision

On the basis of this evidence the judge makes his decision. More often than not it is against the defendant. This is not because of any collusion between the judge and the police, but because the judge, faced with choosing between one man's word and another's, is likely to regard the policeman's word as more reliable. The defendant's interest in the outcome of the case is obvious; the policeman's interest, if he has any beyond legitimate law enforcement, is hard to discover. Hence, since it appears that the policeman has nothing to gain by falsehood, it is assumed that he probably speaks the truth. In a more difficult case, as where a conflict of testimony develops between disinterested witnesses or where circumstantial evidence must be appraised or where value judgments are involved, the problem of determining credibility is far more difficult.

Imposing the Sentence

If the defendant's guilt is established, either by plea or by trial, sentence must be imposed. The only guides the judge has for this difficult task are those provided by the statute under which the defendant stands convicted. These, however, ordinarily state only the maximum and minimum limits of punishment. Thus a statute on speeding might provide that, upon conviction, a defendant should be fined not more than $100, or imprisoned in the county jail for not more than sixty days, or both. A wide area of discretion is obviously left to the judge.

At one time punishments were more rigidly prescribed than today. A great many offenses in England carried mandatory penalties, death being a favorite even for minor offenses. Now we believe that the punishment should fit the crime, and, equally important, that it should also fit the offender. Vengeance has given way to reformation and deterrence as the goals of criminal justice, and with this has come a recognition of the fact that a sentence appropriate for one man may be entirely inappropriate for another who has committed the same offense. For example, a $5 fine may mean very little to a rich man but a great deal to a poor man. Hence for each case the judge is entrusted with the responsibility of fixing, within the limits prescribed by statute, a proper sentence in the light of the character of the individual and the circumstances of his offense.

Such is the theory. The fact is that a judge who handles minor cases rarely knows anything about the individual in front of him except as his character may be revealed by his appearance and demeanor, or about the circumstances of his offense except as they may be disclosed on the traffic ticket or in the testimony given at the trial. The consequence is that each judge tends to develop his own pattern of sentencing, customarily giving a $5 or $25 or $100 fine for a given type of offense, with little or no attempt to make it fit the individual case.

This results neither in individualization of punishment nor in equal justice under law. Its tendency, rather, is to result in a situation where an offender's fate depends upon the personality of the judge who happens to hear his case. There are hundreds of judges hearing the same type of case. Rarely is there any appellate or administrative supervision over them or even communication between them. The consequence is that in the final stage of a traffic case, as in the initial phase of arrest, individual reactions tend to supplant impersonal rules. Rules exist, and they are important, but they are administered by human agencies—sometimes all too human.

Chapter / Three

A Robbery
Prosecution

In this chapter we are concerned with a more serious criminal case involving the possibility of a substantial term of imprisonment or other severe punishment. Attention is focused on a robbery case, but the principles governing the way it is handled are equally applicable to prosecutions for other serious crimes. We are dealing here with what is commonly called a *felony*, as distinguished from a *misdemeanor* or an *offense*. All three are merely different grades of crime, subject to different penalties. The terms vary in meaning from state to state, but wherever used they express the same general idea: Felonies are the most serious crimes, carrying severe penalties, such as long prison terms, or, in some cases, even death; misdemeanors are less serious, carrying shorter terms of imprisonment or moderate fines; and offenses are comparatively minor, carrying relatively light penalties, usually small fines. Definitions of crime are inevitably somewhat arbitrary, for each legislature has almost unlimited power (subject only to constitutional limitations) to declare what conduct shall be punishable and to prescribe penalties. No man can be punished merely because he is bad in general, but any man can be

38

punished for conduct that has been defined (within constitutional limits, of course) as criminal. While murder, rape,
robbery, arson, and the like are crimes everywhere, wide variations exist from state to state as to the criminality of other
kinds of acts—racial intermarriage, for example, or gambling,
or doing business on Sunday. Many kinds of conduct made
punishable as crimes are morally reprehensible, but others,
like parking in a restricted zone, involve little or no moral
blame.

Let us suppose that on the night of March 27, 1963,
Harry Hall, the proprietor of a small grocery store in Los
Angeles, is held up by a young man who whips out a revolver
and says, "This is a stick-up." The proprietor, his hands above
his head, nods toward the cash register, whereupon the other
man reaches into it, takes the cash amounting to some $75
and leaves.

A police alarm is sent out, and within about three
hours officers in a cruising patrol car arrest Walter Williams,
twenty years of age, and charge him with the crime of robbery. This is the first step in the prosecution.

Starting the Proceedings

Already we can see some similarities and some differences between this case and the traffic case considered in
Chapter Two. There the defendant was merely given a ticket
—an invitation to appear in court (subject to his later being
compelled to appear if the invitation was not heeded)—
whereas here at the outset the accused is physically taken into
custody, by force if necessary. This is the usual way of starting prosecution for a serious crime. A variation, used where
more subtle crimes like embezzlement are involved or where
for some reason it is not feasible quickly to apprehend the
accused, is to have a preliminary investigation by the district
attorney or a grand jury and a formal accusation before a
warrant (a court order) is issued for the arrest of the accused.

One thing that this case and the traffic case have in common is the fact that both require governmental action rather than the purely private action needed to initiate a civil case. This flows from the nature of a criminal proceeding, which is prosecuted on behalf of the public, not solely or even primarily on behalf of any individual. There may be, and frequently is, someone who has been harmed—Harry Hall in this case. Sometimes, however, everyone involved in a crime is a willing participant, as in prostitution and gambling cases. Then only the community is offended.

Even when there is a victim, he does not have power to set the machinery of criminal justice in action. All he can do is register a complaint with the police or the district attorney; thereafter his only role is that of a potential witness who may be called upon to tell what he saw and heard. At least this is so in theory. In fact, there are some instances where the wishes of a victim are given almost controlling weight, as in bad check cases; if the victim doesn't want to prosecute, neither does anyone else.

Technically, however, and practically in most situations, the initial decision whether to prosecute falls to government officials. They may decline to act because an accusation is vindictive or unjustified by the facts or the law, but sometimes they decline to act even where a clear violation is shown. Most criminal codes are so broad that their literal and full enforcement would be insufferable. Frequently the codes contain obsolete provisions—for example, exceptionally stringent Sunday blue laws. Sometimes the codes contain provisions inserted more for the moral indignation they express than for any intended practical effect, like the rules branding as criminal various types of sexual activity that Dr. Kinsey assures us are indulged in by great segments of the population. Most citizens understand this, and consequently the great majority of offenses are never even reported. If reported, they seldom get further than the policeman on the beat or the sergeant at the desk.

Role of the District Attorney

Occasionally a doubtful demand for prosecution reaches the district attorney, who must then exercise his discretion. The resources available to him are limited. There are not enough police to arrest, judges to try, or jails to hold all the people who violate the criminal laws; and even if there were, society would not tolerate total enforcement. Hence the district attorney must and does exercise judgment as to whether to prosecute. Herein lies a grave possibility of abuse, but also the greatest challenge the district attorney faces. Prosecuting a criminal case is relatively easy, with about 90 percent of the cases resulting in pleas of guilty obviating trial completely, and most of the remainder resulting in convictions. Deciding whether to bring a case is another matter, calling for wisdom and entailing grave responsibility.

To a very large extent, the district attorney's discretion is, with his knowledge and consent, exercised by the police. In a perfectly clear case like the one now under consideration, involving armed robbery, the police make an arrest as soon as they can after learning of the crime, without consulting the district attorney. Where time is not so crucial, however, or where the decision to proceed is a more difficult one, the district attorney bears the direct responsibility of decision.

Place of Trial

For reasons explained in the preceding two chapters, the prosecution of Williams will have to take place in a state court in Los Angeles.

This would pose problems if Williams had fled to the neighboring state of Arizona after the crime was committed. In that situation the California police officers probably would not have attempted to arrest him unless they were in hot pursuit, in other words, unless they had virtually caught him in the act and given chase immediately, never stopping. In such circumstances their authority would have been respected beyond the borders of California. In any other circumstances, problems would arise that might well dictate that the arrest should be made by Arizona officers.

If Williams were willing to return voluntarily there would be no difficulty in his being apprehended with or without a warrant, by Arizona or California officers. If he stood on his rights, however, the least he could demand would be to be brought forthwith before a judge of the place where he was apprehended who would inquire into the propriety of the arrest and release him if it was illegal. If the arrest was found legal, Williams could sign a written waiver of further formalities and return voluntarily (though in custody of an officer) to the state charging him with crime; but if he still wanted to stand on his rights, the judge would commit him to jail or admit him to bail (the posting of money or a bond) pending extradition.

Extradition is the name given to the procedure by which a state in which a crime has been committed formally demands from another state the surrender of an individual found there who is charged with that crime. The governor of the first state (California in the case we are supposing) submits a written demand for the man's surrender, accompanied by a formal accusation (an indictment or information) to the governor of the second state. That official then issues a warrant for the man's arrest if he is not already in custody, and he is turned over to an official of the demanding state for transportation back to the scene of the crime to stand trial.

Interstate cooperation ordinarily works smoothly. Every state from time to time is interested in arresting fugitives from its own justice and hence is disposed to cooperate with other states facing similar problems.

Appearance before a Magistrate

In Williams' case no extradition is necessary, since he was apprehended locally. Nevertheless, he is entitled to be brought promptly before a magistrate—a local minor judge, very often the one who tries traffic and similar offenses. He has power to deal with a serious case like Williams' only in a preliminary way, and he does so in much the same fashion as a judge dealing with the extradition of a fugitive from another state. The appearance before the magistrate is supposed to occur as soon as possible after arrest, without any detention by the police for the purpose of interrogating the prisoner. The Supreme Court of the United States is apprehensive about third-degree police methods, and has gone far toward making inadmissible in evidence not only forced confessions but also those obtained by ordinary questioning during detention.

One purpose of the appearance before the magistrate is to fix bail. In all except extremely serious cases, the accused can be released pending trial if he deposits money or posts a bond to insure his appearance at trial. The bail is forfeited if he fails to appear. Its amount is fixed by the magistrate, after hearing a description of the charge, at a figure he believes sufficient to insure the presence of the accused. If the accused cannot post the bail required, he will have to remain in jail. The fixing of bail ordinarily works fairly enough for prosperous defendants (of whom there are few), but sometimes unfairly for indigent defendants (of whom there are many). This is because the magistrate too often lacks the time and facilities to properly investigate the financial resources of the accused, his background, job record, family connections, and other matters necessary for an informed judgment as to the likelihood of his appearing for trial if allowed his liberty until then. Sometimes bail is fixed at an unrealistic figure, more than the defendant can raise or more than is necessary to insure his appearance. Probably many defendants who are now incarcerated pending trial could be released upon their own recognizance—meaning their mere promise to return—if only sufficient time were taken at this stage to learn more about them as people.

At this stage, the accused is probably not represented by a lawyer, for he probably doesn't have the money to hire one or the knowledge to realize that one would be useful. No provision is ordinarily made for court-appointed lawyers in the preliminary stages of prosecution.

Another purpose of the appearance before the magistrate is to inquire whether the accused wants a preliminary hearing. If so, it may be held forthwith, but if either the defendant or the government needs time to prepare for it, it will be scheduled for a later date.

Preliminary Hearing

When a preliminary hearing is desired it is conducted by the magistrate whose job is to inquire whether there is enough evidence to justify holding the accused for trial. This is not a full dress hearing to determine guilt or innocence but only a preliminary inquiry, at which ordinarily only witnesses for the prosecution testify (under oath and subject to cross-examination). In this hypothetical case probably the only witness would be the victim of the robbery, who would be asked to identify Williams and tell briefly what happened. Williams might also make a statement if he wished; but he would not have to, being protected by the constitutional privilege against self-incrimination. Then the magistrate would decide either to release Williams or bind him over for trial in an appropriate court. Here it would be the superior court of California "in and for the County of Los Angeles," a court of general jurisdiction. In another state, it might be a court of a different name, with jurisdiction possibly limited to criminal cases.

Thus we see the second governmental screening of a criminal case, this time by a judicial officer.

Formal Accusation

Assuming the case survives beyond the preliminary hearing, the next step is to make a formal accusation. In about half of the states, this is done by a grand jury, a body of sixteen to twenty-three citizens hearing evidence behind closed doors, under the guidance of the district attorney, and providing the third governmental screening of the case. This action duplicates to a large extent the preliminary hearing before the magistrate. In California and about half of the states, this has seemed a superfluous step, with the result that the grand jury need no longer be used. Instead, the district attorney makes the accusation, which is embodied in a document called an *information,* whereas a similar document produced by a grand jury is called an *indictment.*

An information or indictment does not follow automatically from the magistrate's hearing or the accused's waiver of it. There is time at this point for second thoughts as to the desirability of proceeding further, and time also for negotiating with the accused a plea of guilty to a lesser crime than that originally charged. The reason for accepting a plea to a lesser offense may be insufficient evidence to sustain the greater charge, but equally likely, it may be to cut down the number of trials and to achieve quickly a result that the district attorney feels is appropriate. What is the sense of going through a trial for armed robbery, carrying a maximum penalty of ten years imprisonment (which the judge probably would not impose anyway) when the district attorney is satisfied that the five-year maximum for unarmed robbery, to which the accused is willing to plead guilty, would be sufficient punishment? As the saying goes, "The prosecutor swallows the pistol." District attorneys, especially those in metropolitan centers, are faced with the practical problem of handling an immense amount of business. Since there are not enough courtrooms to hold or judges to try all the people who are arrested, many cases must be and are disposed of upon pleas of guilty.

Whether taking the form of an indictment or an information, the accusation follows a set pattern, alleging that at a certain time and place the accused committed a certain criminal act. The section of the criminal code violated is specified, and the description of the accused's conduct couched in the language of that section. Criminal law, unlike that which governs civil cases, is almost wholly based upon statutory provisions, with consequent easy reference to the relevant rules.

Arraignment

Arraignment takes place in the court that has power to try the offense charged—in this case, the superior court—and consists of reading the information or indictment aloud to the accused and asking him how he pleads. His answer is simply "guilty" or "not guilty." In making it, he is physically present in court. There is no such thing in a criminal case in the United States as a trial *in absentia* of the type known in some nations of Europe, nor is there any default judgment of the kind used in civil cases, whereby a judgment may be entered against the defendant for failing to defend. In a criminal case, if the defendant refuses to plead, a plea of not guilty is entered by the judge, and the prosecution is required to prove its case.

The defendant's plea is oral and general. It is not made under oath, and no legal obligation is imposed upon the accused (such as rests upon the defendant in a civil case) to admit those allegations which he knows to be true. The theory is that he has a right to force the prosecution to prove its case. The plea of not guilty does not disclose particular issues in dispute, but is a blanket repudiation of the charge.

If the accused pleads guilty, as we know happens in

about 90 percent of the cases, the only thing that remains is to impose sentence, just as if he had been convicted after a trial.

For purposes of our discussion, we shall assume that Williams pleads not guilty. The trial itself will take place some time after arraignment. Partly this is because of convenience in scheduling judicial workloads, for if a batch of cases is arraigned on the same day, those which result in pleas of guilty can be scheduled for sentencing in a group (imposing sentence is a brief process), and those which result in pleas of not guilty can be scheduled for trial with some assurance that trial will be really necessary. Another and better reason for delaying trial is to give the accused time to prepare his defense. He is constitutionally entitled to a speedy trial, but if it becomes too speedy it may frustrate his even more important right to a fair trial.

Right to Counsel

One thing to be done at the arraignment, if it has not been done already, is to see that Williams is represented by counsel. At one time in England the defendant in a criminal trial was not entitled to be represented by a lawyer even if he was willing and able to hire him. Constitutional provisions, federal, and state, did away with that attitude for the United States, and gave the accused in all cases the right to employ counsel; and England followed suit.

But a further step was needed: the providing of counsel free of charge if the accused was unable to pay. So far as capital cases (those in which the death penalty may be imposed) are concerned, this step was taken in 1932 by the Supreme Court. In a case involving defendants who were not only indigent but also ignorant, illiterate, and young, the Court held that they were deprived of due process of law if they were not furnished with adequate legal representation free of charge. In 1938 the same idea was extended to non-capital crimes, but again depending upon the circumstances of the particular case. In other words, an indigent defendant was not entitled to free counsel merely because he was being tried for a felony; there had to be "special circumstances." Finally in 1963, the Court removed the "special circumstances" qualification and held that "the mere existence of a serious criminal charge constituted in itself special circumstances requiring the services of counsel at trial." [3]

Most persons accused of crime are poor and ignorant, and many come from unpopular, if not despised, racial or ethnic minority groups. They need lawyers, but they seldom have the means to hire them, so the provision of counsel free of charge is a matter of prime importance. Ideally, legal representation should be available in every case from the time of arrest through final appeal, but thus far the United States Constitution has not been interpreted to require it except during trial and the first stage of appeal and except in "serious" cases. The constitutional decisions do not spell out all the details but leave many to be dealt with by local statutes, practices, and decisions. In some states, representation is by a public defender, a salaried government official; in others, by attorneys appointed *ad hoc* by judges and serving with or without compensation, depending upon local arrangements; in still others, by attorneys employed by legal aid societies supported through private voluntary charitable contributions. The quality of representation, as might be supposed, depends not only upon the individual lawyers involved but also upon the machinery for their employment.

Williams is fortunate, for California has one of the oldest and most fully developed public-defender systems in the nation. If he is indigent, as we shall assume, he is entitled to such representation from the time of his preliminary examination through appeal.

The Jury

Williams' case in all probability will be heard by a jury, for the right to trial by jury is constitutionally guaranteed in all states for serious crimes, and in some states for minor crimes as well. It can be waived even in serious cases, but seldom is.

The trial jury (sometimes called a *petit jury* to distinguish it from the larger *grand jury*) consists of twelve laymen drawn from the community at large. The first step in their selection takes place long before any case in which they are to be used is called for trial, and consists of a jury commissioner or court clerk making up a large list of people who meet minimal qualifications—citizenship, literacy, possession of physical and mental faculties, and so forth. No systematic and intentional exclusion of Negroes or other minority groups is permitted, because that might result in the ultimate packing of a jury called upon to decide the fate of a member of such a group. From the large list, a small number of names is picked by lot, and the individuals are summoned to appear in court for possible service. Then, when a case is called for trial, a few of those present are picked by lot to be examined as to their qualifications to serve in the particular case. The lawyers on both sides question them under oath and "challenge for cause" any who are unfit—as by reason of being related to the defendant or one of the attorneys, or having learned too much about the case from newspapers. Such persons are excused by the judge. Finally both sides are allowed a limited number of *peremptory challenges,* meaning ones for which no reason has to be stated. By these methods, the number of jurors is reduced to twelve, who are then sworn to "well and truly try the matter in issue . . . and a true verdict render according to the evidence."

The Trial

Once the jury has been sworn the prosecuting attorney makes an opening speech to them, outlining the evidence he expects to produce, and the defense counsel is also privileged to make an opening statement, outlining his expected evidence.

Then comes the prosecution's evidence. The prosecuting attorney calls his first witness, who may be the victim of the crime, the arresting officer, or any other person with knowledge to contribute, and that person is questioned as to what he saw and heard. Then follows cross-examination or questioning by the defense counsel in an effort to weaken or throw doubt upon the testimony just given by showing it is affected by bias, or dishonesty, or an inability to observe, remember, or report accurately. Questions asked by either side are subject to objections by the other, in which case the judge must decide upon their propriety in accordance with technical rules of evidence.

After the first witness has completed his testimony (it might even go on to *redirect* and *recross* examination), the next witness for the prosecution is called, and the same process repeated; and so on, until all of the prosecution's witnesses have been questioned by both sides, and the prosecution "rests."

At this point the accused may make a motion for acquittal, raising the question of whether the evidence is sufficient to justify reasonable men in finding a verdict against the defendant. If the judge thinks not, he will grant the motion and the accused will be released, terminating the trial. If he thinks the evidence is sufficient, the case will have to proceed, and the defendant will be given the opportunity to produce any witnesses he desires, to be examined by his lawyer and cross-examined by the opposing lawyer, just like the prosecution witnesses.

A peculiar and important characteristic of evidence in a criminal trial concerns the role of the accused as a witness, already mentioned briefly in Chapter Two. He, of all people, should be expected to know what happened; and it would seem that the simplest and most sensible procedure would be to ask him. This, however, is not permitted in American or English practice, even though it is the heart of a criminal trial in France, Germany, and many other countries. In the United States and England, the accused cannot be called as a witness by the prosecution. Furthermore, in most states no comment can be made by the district attorney about the defendant's failure to take the stand in his own behalf, and the judge will instruct the jury to draw no adverse inference from it, emphasizing the proposition that the accused has no obligation to explain the evidence against him. This is part of the privilege against self-incrimination, guaranteed by state and federal constitutions. The privilege has been the subject of lively debate for over a century, but it is now deeply rooted and likely to remain.

After the defendant has introduced whatever evidence he chooses, he has the opportunity again of moving for a directed verdict of acquittal. This motion is substantially the same as that made at the end of the prosecution's case, the only difference being that now the entire evidence is before the judge for his consideration. Again it calls for the judge's appraisal of the sufficiency of the evidence to warrant reasonable men in finding against the defendant.

Only the defendant in a criminal case can move for a directed verdict, never the prosecution. The fact that there can be only a directed verdict of acquittal, never a directed verdict of conviction, means that the jury has power to acquit a defendant for any or no reason. No matter how clear the facts and the law, no matter how cogent the judge's instructions, a jury is free to act as it sees fit on the total situation in the light of its own conception of justice. The reason for acquittal may be nothing more than the sad eyes of the defendant or the distaste of the jury for the law under which he is being tried.

Is such uncontrolled power in the jury good or bad? Certainly reasonable differences of opinion are possible, but at least two points can be made in favor of the existing practice. First the power can only be exercised in favor of clemency to the accused, never against him, and second, the contemporary sense of the community is brought to bear on the application of abstract rules of law to concrete situations. Blind Justice is the traditional ideal, but there is some debate as to whether the blindfold ought not be removed. On a few courthouses, the Goddess is sculptured without her blindfold.

Final Arguments and Instructions

If the judge does not direct a verdict of acquittal, counsel argue the case to the jury, each lawyer giving his view of the evidence and explaining why he thinks the jury should decide in favor of his side. Sometimes these arguments are impassioned appeals to emotion, sometimes coldly logical analyses, depending upon the case and the lawyers involved. The only restriction is that the arguments keep within the boundaries of the evidence and inferences legitimately to be drawn from it. Considerable latitude is allowed to defense counsel, less to the prosecuting attorney.

Finally come the judge's instructions, sometimes called the *charge,* the main purpose of which is to explain to the jury the law applicable to the case. In England and some courts of the United States, the judge is allowed to summarize the evidence and even express his own views as to the result that ought to be reached, but in California, as in the majority of states, the judge is restricted to talking about the law, for fear that otherwise he would be invading the province of the jury. Furthermore, in California and an increasing number of other states, the instructions are standardized, being found in an officially sanctioned form book, so that they do not vary from case to case or judge to judge. What is told to the jury in Williams' case is exactly the same as what is told to the jury in every other case of armed robbery.

An important part of the charge deals with the burden of proof resting upon the prosecution. The jurors are told that the accused starts out with a presumption that he is innocent and that they cannot convict him unless satisfied of his guilt "beyond a reasonable doubt." These words have never been satisfactorily defined, but they somehow convey the idea that the task of the jury is a solemn one, that it should be performed with great care, that life or liberty is at stake. That thought is further reinforced by the requirement in almost every state—also expressed to the jury at this time —that its verdict must be unanimous.

Jury Deliberations

We know little about jury deliberations for they are always carried on behind closed doors. In one sense it seems they must be broad in scope because the jurors have the power, already described, to disregard the law completely; in another sense, they must be narrow because the jurors are restricted to the question of whether the accused is guilty or not guilty, and they are not concerned with what punishment, if any, should be meted out to him. In some states, with respect to some crimes, the jury is given power to recommend, sometimes even to fix, the punishment, as where the choice is between death and life imprisonment; but this is the exception rather than the rule, and not applicable in Williams' case. Of course, the jury can prevent punishment completely by finding Williams not guilty, but if they find him guilty, the sentence is normally for the judge alone to give.

Motion for a New Trial

If the jury finds Williams guilty, his lawyer can move for a new trial, to be granted or denied in the discretion of the judge, depending upon whether he thinks there has been a miscarriage of justice. If the verdict is not guilty, that is the end of the case, for the prosecution can make no equivalent move. The thought here is the same as that governing the motion for a directed verdict: The jury should have an absolute power to acquit without interference by the judge, reinforced by the notion that it would be unfair to put the accused in jeopardy for the second time. Once acquitted, he is free for good.

Sentencing

If Williams is found guilty, and if no new trial is ordered (or if he pleaded guilty), all that remains to be done in the trial court is to sentence him.

As already indicated, this is the job of the judge, probably the most important one that he is called upon to perform, and one whose difficulties have been suggested in the preceding chapter. The judge in Williams' case has a more awesome responsibility than the judge handling a traffic case, because he has a wider range of discretion, attended by more serious consequences. On the other hand, he is helped by the fact that he is likely to know more about the defendant as a human being—his home background, schooling, education, job record, intelligence, previous criminal career. Some of that information is revealed during the trial and some of it is provided by presentence reports, based upon investigations made by probation officers. But after the facts are known the basic problems still remain. When the choice is between death and life imprisonment, which shall be imposed? Or where the choice is less dramatic, should the defendant be let off with a fine, or placed on probation, or given ten years?

The difficulties are complicated by the fact that the goals of criminal law are imperfectly understood. What is the purpose of sentencing? Is it to reform the individual? to deter others from following his example? to protect society? to wreak vengeance upon one who has offended community mores? Such questions have long been asked, but not yet satisfactorily answered; and in the meantime, a judge must proceed according to his own lights, dim and flickering though they be.

Little wonder that great disparity in sentencing is found between one judge and another! Hence it is not surprising that in California and a few other states the sentencing power has to a degree been withdrawn from the judges and vested in another governmental agency where the services of psychiatrists and sociologists are available. Here a decision as to the length of imprisonment does not have to be made until there has been an opportunity to observe the person's conduct and attitudes in prison. Thus, when a California judge sentences a man to the state penitentiary, he does not fix the term of imprisonment, but gives instead what is called an *indeterminate sentence*. An administrative agency then determines, within the statutory limits fixed for the offense—say five years to life—when he shall be released.

Ordinarily sentences are not subject to appellate review except for technical errors, as where the judge has overstepped statutory boundaries. As for the central problem of how discretion in sentencing should be exercised, that is for the trial court alone in most states, California included. In a few states, notably Connecticut, a start has been made toward appellate review of the discretionary element in sentencing, and other jurisdictions are considering the possibility. The object is to secure consistency, so that a man's fate will not depend so much upon which judge happens to sentence him. At the present time, however, this type of review is the exception, and most appellate courts refuse to tackle the problem at all, even for the limited purpose of securing consistency. One reason probably is that they feel that they don't have the answers either; another may be their reluctance to act on the basis of a cold written record without having seen or heard the man whose future is being decided. It seems too much like a doctor prescribing over the telephone for a patient he has never seen.

A recent development that may help to achieve greater uniformity is the practice of holding sentencing institutes, affairs at which judges get together to discuss their common problems, sometimes getting down to concrete cases and trading ideas as to what sentences would be appropriate in given circumstances.

Juvenile Proceedings

If Williams were under eighteen years of age at the time of the commission of the crime (in some other states, sixteen), his case would be handled far differently. He would be treated as a ward of the juvenile court (a specialized branch of the superior court) and when taken into custody would be held in special detention facilities different from those used for adults. His parents would be notified, and he might be released in their custody without bail pending an investigation of the charge by case workers employed by the court. There would still be a hearing, though not the type of trial used for adults. The public is excluded during a juvenile hearing and there is no jury. The proceedings are very informal, though the accused juvenile has the right to be represented by counsel. Upon the conclusion of the hearing, the judge decides not whether the youth is guilty or not guilty, but whether he is a juvenile delinquent, and if adjudged to be such, appropriate treatment for him would be prescribed, which could include his confinement in an institution for the training and rehabilitation of similar young offenders. The proceedings do not leave a permanent black mark on the youth's record, for he would not—in theory at least—have been "convicted" of a "crime."

Postconviction Proceedings

We shall not at this point consider what happens to Williams after he is sentenced except in an extremely general way. One possibility, discussed in detail later, is that he may take an appeal; another is that he will be pardoned or his sentence reduced by the governor; the third is that he will be released on parole long before the expiration of his sentence. Sentences do not ordinarily mean what they say, for prisoners

get time off for good behavior and frequently, if not customarily, are released by parole boards before they have served
their full terms. They are then still subject to mild supervision for a limited period of time by parole officers, but
otherwise free to go their own ways.

Chapter / Four

A Bill Collection

Just as we found it useful to look at a traffic offense case before studying more serious criminal prosecutions, so also here we start with a small bill collection case as a prologue to the consideration of more important civil cases.

Let us suppose that Pablo Peters is a television repairman in Cold Spring, New York, who has fixed the set of his fellow townsman, Neville Norman. The bill is $50, but Norman, though repeatedly asked to pay it, has failed to do so. Peters' patience is exhausted and he decides to sue. He goes to a local justice of the peace to start his action.

Peters could not go to a federal court because his claim is for less than $10,000 and does not involve either a federal question or diversity of citizenship between the parties. He does not go to a higher state court for several reasons. First, they ordinarily entertain only claims for larger amounts; second, their procedure is unduly complicated for a case of this kind entailing unnecessary expense; and third, none is conveniently located from Peters' point of view.

Had the parties lived in New York City, some sixty miles to the south, the case would have gone into the Civil

Court of the City of New York, a court manned by full-time, professional judges, but nevertheless handling small claims. In Cold Spring, such claims are handled by either of two justices of the peace. One is a lawyer, who devotes part of his time to law practice and part (the smaller portion) to his judicial duties. The other is a building contractor, untrained in the law professionally, who is also a part-time judge. Peters' case may be brought before either of them.

Since this is a civil action, unlike a criminal prosecution, it does not have to be brought at the place where the events giving rise to it took place. It does, however, have to be brought where one or the other of the parties resides. This is a rule of *venue,* designed for the convenience of litigants. In this situation both parties live in Cold Spring and that becomes the place of suit.

The Summons and Its Use

Peters probably comes to the justice of the peace alone, for he is likely to consider the matter simple enough to handle himself and too small to justify the expense of engaging a lawyer. If he wants a lawyer, he may employ one of course, to do what otherwise he has to do for himself, namely, at this stage of proceedings, merely to have a summons issued. If Peters is unrepresented, this is done by the justice of the peace (or his clerk, if he has one) upon receipt of a small fee and upon hearing enough about the case to know that it is within the jurisdiction of the court. The justice does not at this point go into the merits of the claim. That is not presently his concern, for the claimant, being entitled to his day in court, cannot be refused an opportunity to present his claim. If Peters is represented by a lawyer, the lawyer may issue the summons with the same effect as if it were issued by the justice—a circumstance that emphasizes the private character of civil litigation. The government is not interested beyond providing machinery for the enforcement of just claims.

The summons is a document that performs a similar (though not identical) function in a civil case to that performed by a ticket in a minor criminal case. The summons notifies the defendant that he is being sued and fixes a time for him to appear in court if he wishes to resist the claim made against him. That time must be not less than six nor more than thirty days after the summons is delivered to the defendant.

The summons contains no statement of the claim, but only notice to the defendant of the time fixed for his appearance in court and an indication of the remedy sought against him—namely, a money judgment for the amount of his debt, with interest and costs.

When the summons is issued, it is put into the hands of the local constable for service. (This means that for a fee the constable delivers the document to the defendant personally.) Different methods of service are possible in other situations and other courts, but we shall postpone consideration of them until we reach more complicated civil actions in the next chapter. When service has been made, the constable fills out a certificate so stating, which appears on the reverse side of the summons.

A Default Judgment

Mr. Norman will probably not contest the claim. The likelihood is that he has no defense, and that his only reason for failing to pay is that he is short of funds. The vast majority of small claims are uncontested. But Norman may and probably will at this point get in touch with his creditor and make arrangements to pay the debt at a later date or in installments.

Norman, however, is not obliged to do anything. He is under no compulsion to appear in court, as he would be if he were being prosecuted for a criminal offense. If he is absent on the return day (the date fixed in the summons for his appearance), that fact will be noted, and judgment will be entered for the plaintiff. There will be no trial because the defendant has tacitly admitted his liability and thus obviated the need for proof.

The judgment is a formal, legal determination, entered on the justice's docket, that the defendant owes a specified sum of money to the plaintiff, together with interest and costs—mainly out-of-pocket expenses of the plaintiff in prosecuting the action. Not included, however, are attorney's fees even if they have been incurred in substantial amount. In the United States we do not, generally speaking, subscribe to the English philosophy that the loser should pay the legal expenses of the winning side. Only in special situations (divorce actions and a few others) or where the losing party has agreed in advance to pay attorney's fees are they recoverable.

The judgment, be it noted, is not an order directing the defendant to pay, but only a determination that he owes the money. Something further needs to be done before the plaintiff is satisfied, either voluntary payment by the defendant or "execution" against his property.

At this point, if he has not already done so, Mr. Norman will probably pay or make arrangements to pay, for otherwise he is asking for trouble. He is not in any danger of being put into jail, for he has committed no crime and violated no order of the court, but he is in danger of losing some of his property.

The simplest form of execution (which is all that we are concerned with here) consists of the local constable seizing enough of the defendant's property to pay the judgment. If there is cash lying around, of course that is taken first. If there is a bank deposit, that is taken by means of an order directing the bank to pay so much of the defendant's deposit to the plaintiff as is needed to satisfy the judgment. If no money or bank account can be found, the constable seizes personal property (meaning movable articles, not real estate). Some types of personal property are exempt from execution, including the tools of the defendant's trade, his family Bible, a reasonable amount of clothing and household utensils for his family, and similar necessities of life.

If the defendant has an automobile, however, or some other form of personal property not exempt from execution (such as a tractor or a boat), that can be seized. It will then be sold at public auction by the constable, who will remit to the justice of the peace (for transmittal to the plaintiff) enough of the proceeds to satisfy the judgment and return the excess to the defendant.

If neither money nor personal property can be found sufficient to satisfy the judgment, the defendant's wages can be garnisheed. This means that the constable, under the direction of the justice of the peace, will order his employer to pay 10 percent of the defendant's wages, due or to become due, directly to the plaintiff until the judgment is satisfied.

To be satisfied along with the judgment are the additional costs incurred since its rendition, namely the fees paid to the constable for executing the judgment. Formerly the fees collected by the justice of the peace (for issuing the summons) and the constable (for serving it and for executing judgment) were retained by them as their compensation. Now, in New York and most states, these officers are paid salaries, and the fees collected by them are turned over to the town by which they are employed.

The Trial

If the defendant wishes to contest the claim, he appears in court on the return date fixed on the summons. At this time, both parties will be asked to *plead*, or state their respective contentions. They ordinarily will do so orally, the plaintiff stating the grounds of his claim, and the defendant the grounds of his defense. Then one side or the other may wish an adjournment before producing evidence. If so, it will be granted, and a future date fixed for trial; if not, the trial will take place immediately.

The trial will be devoted to receiving evidence. Some of it may be documentary (like the bill sent by the plaintiff to the defendant and any correspondence that may have passed between the parties), but most of it will consist of oral testimony. The plaintiff will be sworn to testify truthfully and will tell his story. He may be cross-examined (questioned) by the defendant or his attorney if he has one. Then other witnesses for the plaintiff, if any, will testify. After the plaintiff's witnesses have testified and been cross-examined, the defendant and any witnesses he calls in his behalf will be examined and cross-examined in the same fashion.

At the conclusion of all the evidence, the justice of the peace will decide who wins. If his decision is in favor of the defendant, the case will be dismissed. If it is in favor of the plaintiff, judgment will be entered for him, to be enforced in the same way that a default judgment, described earlier, is enforced.

The foregoing account is of a simple, routine case. A complicated case in a justice of the peace court might involve written pleadings, difficult questions of law, jurisdictional difficulties, and the like, and would be conducted in much the same manner as a case in a court of superior jurisdiction, to be described in the next chapter. A fact that should be mentioned here, however, is that trial by jury is possible, and constitutionally guaranteed in some states, even in a trifling civil case. Considering that some criminal offenses involving far greater stakes are not so triable, this is remarkable, even shocking as a revelation of the values historically placed upon property rights as distinguished from personal rights. The right to trial by jury in small civil cases, however, is hardly ever claimed—a triumph of the good common sense of litigants.

Chapter / Five

A Personal Injury Case

As a preamble to the consideration of a more serious kind of civil case, a few remarks are in order on the nature of civil liability in general as compared and contrasted with criminal responsibility.

A single incident may give rise to both a civil claim and criminal prosecution. If a man, driving his car while drunk, kills a pedestrian, he may be guilty of homicide and also liable in damages to the pedestrian's widow. Two separate proceedings, however, will be necessary to enforce his two distinct responsibilities, neither of which will depend upon the other. The government may (or may not) prosecute the man criminally and may or may not succeed; but whatever it does and with whatever success, the widow's claim will not be affected. She must bring a civil action for damages, which will be governed by different rules and conducted according to different procedures. Neither she nor the defendant will ordinarily be allowed even to disclose in this proceeding the result reached in the other.

In the United States, we have no such procedure as that which prevails in France and some other countries, called *adhesion.* Under this procedure, when a single event gives rise to both civil and criminal liability the injured party is allowed to assert his claim in the criminal prosecution, abiding the event. This saves the necessity of two separate trials and complicates the criminal prosecution only to the extent of adding the issue of damages. Wisely or unwisely, the United States has not seen fit to adopt this procedure and so separate proceedings are necessary in such situations.

Civil claims do not always, or even ordinarily, arise out of criminal activities. Usually they result from conduct that is not criminal. Thus a man who breaks his contract with another or who injures him negligently has committed no crime, but only a civil wrong. For this he may be sued civilly by the injured party, not prosecuted criminally by the government.

The Area of Civil Liability

The range of civil wrongs is broad. It includes injuries recognized by legislatures as justifying individual redress, as where a statute provides that a wife may get a divorce because of her husband's desertion or that a tenant may recover overcharges of rent from a landlord, yet goes far beyond them. Most of our law defining civil responsibility, unlike our criminal law, is not statutory. It is the judge-made common law described in Chapter One.

The list of civil wrongs is not unlimited, any more than is the catalogue of criminal offenses. There are many grievances for which the law provides no redress (breaches of etiquette and even some breaches of morals) just as there are certain kinds of morally blameless conduct that are prohibited by law. While the area of law overlaps that of morals to a very large extent, their boundaries are not coterminous. A man may be morally obligated to help a stranger in distress or to carry out his promise to make a gift but not legally bound to do so. And he may be morally free to engage in activities that nevertheless may result in his legal liability without any fault on his part—blasting, for example, which, though conducted with all reasonable care, injures the property of another. In short, the range of civil wrongs in law is defined by what judges and legislators have done in providing civil sanctions against certain kinds of conduct and not against others.

The range of civil remedies is also broad, though again not unlimited, and again the ones available are largely the product of history. The most frequently used civil remedy is a money judgment for damages, but there are others that are also common. One is the injunction, ordering the defendant to do or refrain from doing a certain act upon penalty of being thrown into jail until he complies. Another civil remedy is taking away from the defendant and awarding to the plaintiff property to which the defendant has no right; if the defendant balks, the sheriff or other law-enforcement officer can take it away from him by force. Still another is a declaration of the rights or status of the parties, as a divorce decree dissolving a marriage; here no enforcement is needed for the judgment itself accomplishes the desired result.

The object of a civil action is to secure any one of these or other recognized remedies (we shall mention more as the discussion proceeds). Whether one will be given depends upon whether it is permitted under the rules of substantive law as applied to the facts of the case.

An Auto Accident

With this background, we are in a position to consider a claim for damages for personal injuries—a very common type of case. Important in its own right, it also furnishes a key to the understanding of how other substantial civil cases are handled.

Let us assume that Caleb Carlson, who lives in Detroit, is visiting in Indianapolis. While walking across the street there, he is run over by a car owned and driven by Waldo Walsh, who lives in Chicago. Carlson suffers severe bodily injuries. Upon his release from the hospital and his return home, permanently disabled, he decides to sue.

The first thing he does is hire a lawyer, for this is the type of case that a man ordinarily doesn't attempt to handle for himself. Being a civil case, it is one for which the government will not furnish a lawyer free of charge to either side; and involving the possibility of recovering a substantial sum of money, it is one for which no legal aid society is likely to furnish free legal help. Carlson, therefore, will himself have to find and retain a lawyer. His task will be made easy by the fact that many lawyers are willing to take cases like this upon a *contingent fee*. The arrangement is that Carlson pays nothing if he loses, but a percentage of whatever he recovers to his lawyer—usually 25 percent if the recovery comes by way of an out-of-court settlement and 33⅓ percent if it results from a trial. Legal fees in most litigated cases are contingent in the sense that their amount depends to some extent upon success or failure, and upon the amount of money involved; but in personal injury cases on the plaintiff's side, they are usually wholly contingent, the lawyer taking nothing unless he wins. The defendant's lawyer, on the other hand, is usually compensated on a *per diem* (daily fee) basis.

The plaintiff's lawyer interviews his client, makes an investigation into how the accident happened and the nature and extent of injuries, and possibly does some research into the law. Then he tries to settle the case with the defendant's insurance company, if there is one. Most motorists today are insured against liability, and their policies provide that the insurance company will not only pay any judgment recovered (or such part as is within the policy limits of liability) but also will defend the action and take care of negotiations looking toward settlement. If the claim can be settled at a figure agreeable to both sides, that is the end of the matter. Carlson's lawyer takes his agreed percentage and Carlson gets the rest. The great majority of all claims are settled in this manner.

Let us assume, however, that this case cannot be settled, at least at this stage. Preparations must now be made for suit.

Place of Suit

The first problem is where suit can be brought. If this were a criminal proceeding, it would have to be brought at the place where the events giving rise to it took place—Indiana. But, being a civil case and not involving property, it is *transitory* and can be brought wherever the defendant can be properly served with a summons.

A summons, as we saw earlier in connection with the bill collection case, is a document inviting the defendant to come in and present his side of the story and warning him that if he fails to do so judgment will be rendered against him by default. It is ordinarily good only within the state where the court that issues it sits. Since Walsh lives in Illinois, a summons from a court in Michigan will probably be useless, although there is some possibility that he might visit Michigan and thus be served with the summons. From Carlson's point of view, that would be ideal, for Michigan would be the most convenient place of trial for him. Nevertheless, Carlson's lawyer doesn't dare gamble on that remote chance. Why wait? Besides, the statute of limitations, arbitrarily extinguishing the claim if it is not asserted in court within a certain period of time from the accident, might run out.

Hence the logical place to sue is Illinois. A summons issued from a court there will be relatively easy to serve and unquestionably valid. Illinois happens to have an unusually generous statute on the service of a summons, exploiting to the full the state's constitutional power. It allows service outside of the state upon a nonresident if the claim arose from almost any act taking place within the borders of Illinois. In this case, however, it is not relevant or needed, for the standard, old-fashioned type of personal service within the state where the action is brought can be accomplished easily in view of Walsh's local residence.

Another possible place would be Indiana, where the accident took place. Like most states it has a nonresident motorist rule, which allows a summons to be served outside of its borders in an action arising from an auto accident that took place within its borders with the same effect as a summons served locally. The defendant must heed it or judgment will be entered against him by default. There is, of course, no extradition in a civil case since the presence of the defendant is not necessary. In this situation, and some others having no relevancy to it, the usual rule that a summons is invalid beyond the borders of the state where issued is relaxed. But Indiana is no more convenient for Carlson or his lawyer than Illinois. Hence we shall assume that the decision is made to sue in Illinois.

State Court or Federal Court?

Still to be decided is the question of which court in Illinois is appropriate. There are two possibilities: a state court of general jurisdiction (a justice-of-the-peace-type court or one exercising only criminal jurisdiction would obviously be inappropriate) or the federal district court in Chicago. This case satisfies the requirements of federal jurisdiction mentioned earlier: it involves more than $10,000 in controversy (we may safely assume that Carlson's lawyer will not be suing for less than that) and it is between citizens of different states. This case is not based upon federal law, but for reasons explained earlier that is not necessary.

The choice between a state and a federal court cannot be made upon the difference of any realistically anticipated difference in result. A federal court in Illinois is required to apply the same substantive law as would be applied by the courts of the state in which it is sitting. In this case that would probably be the law of Indiana where the accident happened. This is in accordance with the traditional view that rights and duties arising out of a given event ought to be fixed by the law governing the place where the event takes place and ought not to depend upon where suit happens to be brought. In a case of this kind, there would not likely be any very great difference between the substantive law of Indiana and that of Illinois, so that even if Illinois were disposed to depart from the traditional view and apply its own rules to an event occurring outside its borders (to the extent that it could constitutionally do so), the result probably would not be affected.

Procedural law, however, is another matter, pertaining, as it does, to the mechanics of litigation—how a summons is served, what pleadings are required, what evidence is admitted, and the like. Each jurisdiction uses its own procedural rules, regardless of the kind of claim being tried or the substantive rules that govern it. Hence, an Illinois state court will use Illinois procedure, and a federal court will use federal procedure, neither worrying about the procedural rules of Indiana. To attempt to do otherwise would be impossibly complicated and burdensome.

If Carlson's lawyer prefers Illinois procedure over federal procedure, or vice versa, that would be a legitimate basis for his choosing one court over the other. Other factors of choice are less easily defined: the personalities of judges (hard to estimate because there are several judges in each court and it is impossible to guess in advance which would get the case); the jurors likely to be picked (those who would serve in the state court would be chosen from the city of Chicago whereas those who would serve in the federal court would be chosen from the federal district, a somewhat larger area); the conditions of the calendars in the two courts (one court may be much further behind in its work than the other, so Carlson's case would have to wait longer for trial).

Let us assume that for one or more of the reasons mentioned, Carlson's lawyer decides to institute suit in the federal court. He may decide to retain local counsel in Illinois or to handle the case himself. Being a Michigan lawyer, licensed to practice only there, he does not have the right to practice in Illinois, even in a federal court. But there is no real difficulty, for he may be admitted on the motion of a local lawyer as a matter of courtesy for the purpose of handling this one case.

The Complaint

The problem now is to get the action under way. As a condition of having a summons issued that may be served on Walsh, Carlson's lawyer must file a *complaint*, which is a document stating briefly Carlson's version of what happened between him and Walsh and concluding with a request for an appropriate remedy. It serves the same purpose for a civil case as an information or indictment in a criminal case.

Not much detail is provided in the complaint as to how the accident happened or the injuries suffered, only a bare outline of *who* was involved, *what* happened, *when*, *where*, and *why* (Walsh's negligence). Law is not mentioned, but is implicit in the background, for the facts alleged are those which under the governing substantive law entitle Carlson to the remedy he seeks against Walsh. If the word "negligently" (or another expression conveying the same idea) were omitted, the complaint would not be good, because the law of Indiana does not make a motorist responsible for injuries suffered in a collision unless he is at fault. The judgment asked is damages, which is the only remedy appropriate under the circumstances.

The complaint is filed in the clerk's office of the federal court, which thereupon issues a summons. This is mandatory, for the clerk's office has no right to question the validity of the claim or the propriety of the complaint. If any such questions are to be raised, they must be raised by the defendant. This being a civil claim, the government has no interest in it except to furnish a forum for its assertion and fair rules for the resolution of whatever controversy develops between the parties. The summons will be substantially similar to that seen earlier in the bill collection case and will be served in substantially the same manner, though by a United States marshal rather than the town constable.

Defendant's Response

The next move is up to the defendant. If he does nothing, judgment will be entered against him by default substantially in the manner described in Chapter Four. The only difference is that here an inquiry (by a jury or by a judge alone, in his discretion) will be necessary as to the amount of damages, for they are not *liquidated*—susceptible of accurate mathematical measurement—like those involved in a suit on a promissory note. A demand (say for $100,000) in the complaint is nothing more than a guess (or a hope) on the part of the plaintiff's lawyer as to what a jury might award for not only such measurable items as doctors' and hospital bills and lost wages but also for such incalculable items as pain, suffering, and loss of future earnings. Hence the inquiry before entering judgment. The defendant is duly notified of it and given an opportunity to present evidence, which, however, is limited to the question of damages; he is not permitted to introduce evidence on the question of liability, for that has been admitted by the default.

In Carlson's case, the defendant is going to resist the claim, as we know from the fact that his insurance company has been engaged in unsuccessful negotiations for settlement. While Walsh is named and served as the defendant and will probably have to testify as a witness, the insurance company is at least as much concerned as he. The reason it is not named as a defendant is that its policy provides only that it will pay (up to policy limits) any *judgment* rendered against *Walsh*.

The defendant can resist the claim as a matter of law (by moving to dismiss the complaint on the ground that the facts alleged are not legally sufficient to justify a remedy) or as a matter of fact (by disputing in his answer the plaintiff's version of the facts), or on both grounds.

Motion to Dismiss

Had Carlson sued the insurance company instead of Walsh, the proper defense tactic would have been a motion to dismiss the complaint. That would have presented to the judge the question of whether the facts alleged in the complaint, if true, justified the relief sought, namely a judgment against the insurance company. For reasons already suggested, Carlson has no legal basis for suing the insurance company directly. It did not cause his injuries, nor did it contract with him to pay for them. Arguably, Carlson was the intended beneficiary of the contract between the company and Walsh, but even so, the event that would make the company liable—a judgment against Walsh—had not yet occurred, so that a motion to dismiss such a complaint would have been sustained.

Such a motion can be used whenever the defendant contends that the allegations of the plaintiff, taking them at face value and assuming them to be true, do not entitle him to a remedy against the defendant. The issue presented is one of law: Do the alleged facts justify relief? It is decided by the judge, solely upon the basis of the pleadings and arguments of the lawyers and without any trial to determine if the allegations are true or false; for they are assumed to be true. If the judge grants the motion, the case is dismissed (subject to the possibility of the plaintiff submitting an amended complaint); but if he denies it, the defendant has an opportunity to answer the complaint, raising issues of fact that ultimately may have to go to trial.

The Answer

Since in Carlson's case there is no basis for a successful motion to dismiss, we shall assume that Walsh proceeds to submit an *answer*, which, like the complaint, is a *pleading*, containing the defendant's version of the facts. It has no close counterpart in a criminal case (where the defendant orally pleads guilty or not guilty), for this is a written document, submitted well in advance of trial, in which the defendant is required not only to be specific, but also honest in disclosing his position. He admits or denies what the plaintiff has alleged, and in addition states any other facts that, in his view, defeat the claim. If, for example, the defendant had paid money in settlement of the claim and received a release of liability, he would allege this. The plaintiff would then be privileged to attack the legal sufficiency of the defendant's allegations by a motion to strike them from the answer, thus raising the same kind of legal question as the motion on the part of the defendant to dismiss the complaint: Do the allegations, assuming they are true, defeat the claim as a matter of law? If the plaintiff did not raise any such legal question, he would be deemed to dispute the allegations, allowing him at the trial to introduce any evidence that would tend to contradict or avoid them.

Whether the answer contains only denials or only affirmative defenses of the kind just described or both, factual issues are presented which normally are expected to be resolved by trial.

A Counterclaim

Included in the answer may be a *counterclaim*, which, as its name suggests, is a claim asserted by the defendant against the plaintiff. It need not, though it usually does, arise out of the same transaction that gives rise to the plaintiff's claim, in which case it must be asserted in the same case or else waived. If in the accident now under consideration, Walsh himself had suffered personal injuries or property damage, and if he claimed that they were due to Carlson's fault, he would assert his claim as a counterclaim. In that event, Carlson would have to submit a further pleading, called a *reply* in which he in effect answered the counterclaim, admitting or denying its allegations. Again a trial normally would be necessary to resolve the dispute.

Procedure before Trial

Trial, however, is some time away. It is notorious how long litigants must sometimes wait for trial. In some courts, the interval between the time a case is at issue and when it is reached for trial is as much as five years. Much time, thought, and money have been devoted to trying to eliminate the law's delay, but the problem still persists.

While awaiting trial, either side may move for *summary judgment*. This motion, to be decided by the judge without a trial and without a jury, can be used only in a very clear case, where there is no genuine dispute of fact and where the allegations in the pleading of one of the parties are demonstrably false. It would be a useful technique in a routine bill collection case where the plaintiff had indisputable documentary proof of the bill and the defendant's failure to pay, but it can be of no help in the Carlson case, where there is a genuine dispute as to whose negligence caused the accident.

More useful in this case would be *discovery*. This is the name given to a collection of devices that allow the parties to investigate evidence in preparation for trial. Either party could question the other or any third person, orally or in writing, outside of court and with a minimum of formality. Either could get a court order permitting him to inspect and photograph or copy documents or things relevant to the controversy in the possession of the other party. The defendant could have his doctor give the plaintiff a physical examination as to the nature and extent of his injuries. Either side could demand admissions from the other as to the genuineness of relevant documents or particular matters of fact. These techniques, so useful in preventing surprise at the trial and in getting away from the sporting theory of justice (in which legal skills and maneuvers become disproportionately important in determining the outcome) are ironically not available in criminal cases when the interests at stake are far greater.

When discovery is complete, both lawyers will probably be called for a pretrial conference with the judge. While there are many variations from one court to another as to how and in what situations this device is used, the general idea is that the judge and the two lawyers talk the case over, trying to settle it if possible, but if not, to streamline it for trial by agreeing as to matters not in dispute and defining as precisely as possible the remaining issues.

The Trial

If the case cannot be settled (about 90 percent of personal injury actions are settled before trial), trial is necessary. It follows in general the same pattern as a trial in a criminal case, but with some important differences about to be noted.

The parties may or may not be entitled to trial by jury. The right exists only for actions *at law* not for suits *in equity*. The difference is historical, actions at law being those which developed in the King's Bench, Common Pleas, or Exchequer courts of England, and suits in equity being those which developed in the English Court of Chancery. American constitutional provisions typically provide that the right to trial by jury shall "remain inviolate," which has been interpreted to mean that the right was preserved in those kinds of cases in which it had theretofore been enjoyed but not extended to those where it had not been enjoyed. Carlson's case is an action at law and consequently one side or the other might and probably would have demanded a jury. That should have been done in the pleading stage of the case, or else the right was waived, so that if both sides had been willing to dispense with it (or neglectful), the judge might have tried the case without a jury.

Motions during trial in a civil case differ somewhat from those in a criminal case. There, it will be recalled, only the defendant could move for a directed verdict of acquittal or a new trial after conviction. In a civil case, either side can move for a directed verdict, which will be granted if the evidence is so clear that reasonable men could reach only one result; either side can also move for a new trial after an adverse verdict. The civil jury, therefore, is more limited than the criminal in taking the law into its own hands. In another sense, however, it has greater power than the criminal jury, for it not only decides who wins but also, if the plaintiff succeeds, how much he receives. In a criminal case, it will be recalled, the jury normally decides only guilt or innocence and has nothing to do with the sentence.

In a civil case, the defendant is not privileged from taking the witness stand as he is in a criminal case, but may be called and examined by the plaintiff. The privilege against self-incrimination, while not entirely irrelevant in a civil case, is rarely invoked.

The burden of proof is different too. It is not necessarily all on the plaintiff, for once he has established the essential elements of his claim, the defendant may have the burden of convincing the jury as to his affirmative defense or his counterclaim. Furthermore, the burden is not so heavy—"a preponderance of the evidence" rather than proof "beyond a reasonable doubt" is the test. The distinction is difficult to define, but nevertheless real, for the words "preponderance of the evidence" somehow convey to the jury that they are dealing with interests less vital than the life or liberty that is at stake in a criminal trial. Reinforcing the thought that less caution is demanded in a civil trial case than in a criminal trial is the fact that in many states a civil verdict can be rendered without unanimous agreement among the jurors. In the federal court where Carlson's case is being tried this is not so, for unanimity is required by the United States Constitution; but in some states, governed in this respect by state rather than federal constitutional provisions, five sixths or three fourths of the jurors can render a civil verdict.

Another divergence between federal and state practice concerns the nature of the judge's instructions. In a federal court, and hence in Carlson's case, the judge may comment on the evidence, summarizing it and giving the jury the benefit of his opinion. He may be reluctant to do so in the ordinary case, preferring not to influence the jury, but he has the power if he wishes to exercise it. In many state courts, as we saw in Chapter Three, comment on the facts by the judge is prohibited, his role being limited to an explanation of the law governing the case.

Except in the respects noted, a civil trial follows the same pattern as a criminal trial.

Judgment and Execution

Judgment, instead of imposing punishment such as a fine or imprisonment, awards a civil remedy appropriate to the circumstances—in this case money damages. It is enforced in much the same way that a judgment for money in a minor court on a small claim is enforced. The defendant is not ordered to pay but if he fails to do so voluntarily his property will be seized and sold on execution.

The defendant may, however, not have any property that is locally available. In that case, the judgment can be enforced in a state other than that where it was rendered. Suppose, for example, Walsh had no insurance to pay the judgment, and he owned some property located in Florida. Since the judgment in this case had been entered by a federal court, the procedure would be simple. The judgment would be registered in the federal district court where the property was located and enforced as though it had been rendered by that court.

If necessary, the defendant could be examined under oath to discover the nature and location of his assets. The job of enforcement would be done by a United States marshal, but he would have to operate in accordance with local state rules regarding the methods used and the property subject to seizure.

If the original judgment had been rendered by a state court, interstate enforcement would have been slightly more difficult. A new action would have had to be brought, based on the original judgment, in a state where property of the defendant could be found. The second court would not retry the original claim, but at most it would inquire—upon the initiative of the defendant—into the question of whether the first court had jurisdiction. If it decided against the first court, the second court could disregard the judgment, treating it as an absolute nullity. If the first court was found to have had jurisdiction, however, the second court would have no alternative but to respect the judgment, right or wrong, and to enter its own judgment to the same effect, to be enforced according to local procedure. This is an example of the doctrine of *res judicata*—there can be no relitigation on the merits of a case decided by a court having jurisdiction—reinforced by the requirement of the United States Constitution that every state court give "full faith and credit" to valid judgments rendered by the courts of sister states.

Chapter / Six

A Divorce Case

A divorce case follows the pattern of other civil cases to a considerable extent, but there are important differences. These are worth noting, especially since divorce litigation is so common and affects so many people.

Let us suppose that Philip and Pamela Powers, who are residents of New York City, are unhappily married. They have two children, a pleasant apartment, and a good income (Philip is an executive earning $20,000 a year), but they think they have nothing in common. In fact, both regard their marriage as intolerable. Philip drinks excessively and has a roving eye, according to Pamela; and Pamela, according to Philip, is a nonstop nagger whose housekeeping leaves much to be desired. They decide to get a divorce, and Pamela goes to consult a lawyer.

Conciliation Attempts

Had the parties been in less fortunate circumstances financially, Pamela might have gone to the family court in

New York (which is a *social* court not unlike the juvenile court described in Chapter Two). The family court would have sent her to its conciliation service where a marriage counsellor—not a lawyer but a psychologist or social worker employed by the court—would have attempted to patch up the marriage through interviews with husband and wife, separately or together. Had such efforts succeeded, the divorce could have been averted, or at least postponed.

Since the Powers have money, Pamela consults a lawyer. As a conscientious man he will attempt, if he thinks there is any chance of success, to do the same thing the marriage counsellor would have tried—get the parties back together again. If Philip has a lawyer by this time, negotiations will have to be conducted through him or at least with his help. But perhaps neither of the lawyers will have the necessary skills to reconcile the warring spouses. In any event, we shall assume that they conclude that a divorce is the only solution.

The first problem is where the suit should be brought.

Governing Law

We have observed in earlier chapters that law is not uniform throughout the United States and that, because of the federal system of government, each state has a large measure of autonomy. Nowhere are these principles more clearly exemplified than in the law of domestic relations. The central government has no power to prescribe nationwide rules, so each state makes its own, some allowing easy divorce, others making it next to impossible.

In New York, the sole ground for divorce is adultery. New York law would control the divorce suit if the ordinary rules prevailed, since New York is the place where the parties were married and where they have made their home.

But the ordinary rules do not prevail. In a divorce action, the court applies the law of its own state regardless of where the events giving rise to the suit may have occurred. Hence if the suit can be brought in a state other than New York—say, Nevada—New York's strict laws can be evaded. In Nevada, the grounds for divorce are as follows: (1) Impotence at the time of the marriage continuing to the time of the divorce; (2) Adultery since the marriage, remaining unforgiven; (3) Willful desertion, at any time, of either party by the other, for the period of one year; (4) Conviction of felony or infamous crime; (5) Habitual gross drunkenness contracted since marriage, of either party, which shall incapacitate such party from contributing his or her share to the support of the family; (6) Extreme cruelty in either party; (7) Neglect of the husband, for the period of one year, to provide the common necessaries of life, when such neglect is not the result of poverty on the part of the husband which he could not avoid by ordinary industry; (8) Insanity existing for two years prior to the commencement of the action . . . ; and (9) When the husband and wife have lived separate and apart for three consecutive years without cohabitation the court may, in its discretion, grant an absolute decree of divorce at the suit of either party.

If the Powers prefer to get a divorce in Nevada rather than New York they can hardly be blamed. A New York divorce is a messy affair. If adultery has occurred, it humiliates and embarrasses both parties by the public disclosure of that fact. If it has not occurred, the proceeding is dishonest, involving the manufacture of evidence, either by the deliberate or collusive commission of the act of adultery or by the subornation of perjury.

Another possibility, however, would be an annulment —a proceeding by which a judge dissolves the marriage by declaring that it never existed. The theory is that the marriage is void because one or both of the parties was incapable of entering into the relationship (being underage or already married, for example) or because the consent of one party was procured by fraud (the other party, for example, promising to have children while secretly determined never to try). The available grounds for annulment do not fit the Powers' case, and even if they did the proceedings would be as unsatisfactory and possibly involve as much chicanery as a local divorce. Hence the decision is made to seek a divorce elsewhere.

An Action in Nevada

In most civil actions, the plaintiff sues in a court of the state where the defendant lives. That is because the summons ordinarily has to be served personally in the state where issued.

In a divorce action different considerations apply. For reasons that are too abstruse to explain here, personal service of the summons is not required if the only object of the action is to terminate the marital relationship; publishing it in a newspaper and sending a copy to the defendant by mail is enough. What is required is that the *plaintiff* be *domiciled* in the state where the action is brought, meaning that she reside there with the intention of making it her home. If that is (or appears to be) the situation, she is entitled to sue for divorce regardless of the fact that her husband lives elsewhere. In other words, the usual rules of jurisdiction are turned upside down, for in the ordinary civil action (to collect a debt or recover damages for personal injury) the residence of the plaintiff is immaterial while that of the defendant may be crucial (because of the usual necessity of personally serving the summons upon him).

If the plaintiff-wife seeks alimony as well as a termination of the marriage then the usual rules again come into play. There must be personal service of the summons on the defendant or some equivalent, giving the court the power to render a money judgment against him. That equivalent may be supplied by the defendant's *general appearance*. This means not that he physically enters the court but that he acknowledges its jurisdiction, as by answering the plaintiff's complaint and seeking judgment in his own favor. In the ordinary case an appearance connotes a contest, but in a divorce action it may be nothing more than ritual, performed for the purpose of accomplishing a result earnestly desired by both sides.

The Proceedings

Assuming that the action is launched without mishap, most of Pamela's worries (and those of her husband) are over. While there might be a full-dress, seriously fought trial, the likelihood is that there will be no contest.

Judgment by default, however, is not possible, as it is in the ordinary civil case where the government is disinterested in the outcome. The law takes what some persons regard as a rather perverse attitude toward divorce. It says that a marriage cannot be dissolved by consent of the parties, that if one party wants a divorce, it may be granted, but that if both parties want it, it will be denied on the ground of *collusion*. Another peculiar concept is that the divorce must be based upon one-sided fault. If one spouse has committed adultery the divorce may be granted, but if both have committed adultery it will be denied. In short, the theory is that the state has an interest in preserving marriage and minimizing divorce. However, it falls short of adequately explaining which state—as between New York and Nevada in this case—has the greater interest. Both, we shall see, are involved, but Nevada's involvement comes first. A judge of that state must hear the plaintiff's evidence to make sure that she is entitled to a divorce—that she is a bona fide resident of Nevada, and that her grounds for dissolving the marriage are genuine and adequate. If the action is uncontested, this will not take long —probably no more than ten or fifteen minutes. Then in due course a decree of divorce will be entered, including, in all probability, provisions for alimony as outlined in a *separation agreement* between the parties drafted by their lawyers in New York.

If the action is contested, a full trial may take place,

following the same pattern as in other civil actions. A jury, however, will not be used, for divorce is not one of the actions developed in the common-law courts of England. Until about 1800 an English marriage could be terminated only by act of Parliament. Judicial divorce was developed later, after most American constitutional provisions guaranteeing the right to trial by jury had gone into effect. Since the Constitution merely preserves the right and does not extend it, its provisions have no application to divorce proceedings. Nevada could grant the right by legislation or special constitutional provision (as is done in some states for some types of divorce cases), but it has not seen fit to do so. Hence a divorce trial takes place before the judge alone.

Full Faith and Credit

Assuming that Mrs. Powers is granted a divorce in Nevada, will it be good? Can the parties remarry without the fear of committing bigamy or producing bastards? Will the alimony be collectable?

The answers to these questions depend upon whether the Nevada decree is ever challenged, and, if it is, whether it will be upheld.

Let us assume that Pamela after getting her divorce decides to return to New York. That she is privileged to change her domicile is proved by the fact that she has done so once already. She is not likely to challenge the divorce, having gone to so much trouble to get it. Neither is her husband in the state of mind we have been assuming. Both may remarry and live happily ever after.

But challenge is not beyond the reach of possibility. Conceivably one of the parties may have a change of heart, especially if that seems financially desirable. If Pamela tries to upset the divorce by proceedings in New York she will fail, being bound by her own actions. Should Philip attempt to upset the divorce—for example, when Pamela seeks a New

York judgment for alimony based upon it—he may fail too. If he appeared in the Nevada action, he is also bound by the decree, for he either litigated or had the opportunity to litigate the questions of domicile and jurisdiction and will not be given another opportunity. In other words, a New York court is forced to give full faith and credit to a judgment it would never have entered itself, not because the court which rendered it had jurisdiction, but because none of the parties is in a position to raise the question.

The Nevada divorce could be tested by Philip if he had not appeared or by someone else not bound by the judgment —the State of New York, for example, prosecuting for bigamy. In that case, a court of New York could independently inquire into whether the Nevada court had jurisdiction, whether, in other words, Pamela had established a bona fide domicile in Nevada at the time of the divorce. If it found that the Nevada court lacked jurisdiction, it could disregard the decree, treating it as nugatory and void. If it found, on the other hand, that the Nevada court had jurisdiction, that would have to be the end of the matter. The New York court could not inquire into the merits of the divorce or the adequacy of the grounds for it. It would be required to accord the decree the same full faith and credit required by the Constitution to be given to every other judgment rendered by a court having jurisdiction.

The strongest evidence that a Nevada divorce is accepted in New York is not found in any decision of the Supreme Court of the United States or the New York Court of Appeals but in the fact that in 1962 Mrs. Nelson D. Rockefeller, while her husband was governor of New York, secured a Nevada divorce and returned to New York. Shortly thereafter her former husband was re-elected to his second term of office.

Chapter / Seven

Appellate Review

As we have noted in earlier chapters, not many cases are actually contested. Most criminal prosecutions result in pleas of guilty and most civil actions are settled or defaulted. The relatively few contested cases are likely to be fought vigorously and to result in judgments that leave one side or the other unhappy. When this happens the aggrieved party may want to appeal to a higher court.

No automatic review is provided; it must be sought and initiated by one of the litigants. Appellate courts, like trial courts, are not self-starting mechanisms. The right of appeal, although not constitutionally guaranteed, is provided by legislation for virtually every type of case, large or small, civil or criminal. There is one very important qualification, however: In most states, in a criminal case the government may not appeal. If the defendant has been acquitted that is the end of the matter. Only where there has been a conviction may an appeal be taken and then only by the defendant. In Connecticut and Wisconsin a variation from this theme exists: The government may appeal on a question of law, such as a judge's erroneous instruction, although as in other states, it may not appeal on the basic factual issue of guilt or innocence.

The fact that a litigant may have a right to appeal does not mean that he will take advantage of it. Very few appeals are taken—less than 10 percent on the average—compared to the number of cases tried. Unless there is some reasonable likelihood that the judgment will be reversed, unless, in other words, it is demonstrable that the trial court reached a wrong result on the law or the facts, there is no point in spending further time and money on the litigation. Appeals are expensive as well as time consuming.

Minor Case Appeals

Before considering the ordinary type of appeal we should first look briefly at a special type provided for those minor cases which are tried in justice of the peace courts and similar inferior tribunals. In such cases the aggrieved party—meaning the convicted defendant in a criminal case or either party who has lost in a civil case—is entitled to a retrial in a higher tribunal, one where the judges enjoy greater prestige and where there is more time for deliberation. The retrial takes place in a trial court of superior jurisdiction and follows the same pattern as the trial of a more serious case that is brought there originally. Witnesses are heard in the usual fashion and a jury may even be empaneled. Little or no attention is paid to what transpired at the first trial, for the whole job is done anew as if the first trial had never taken place. This type of proceeding, which is called by lawyers a trial *de novo*, is vastly different, as we shall see, from the ordinary appeal about to be discussed.

Ordinary Appeals

For the more serious civil and criminal cases tried originally in courts of superior jurisdiction, a retrial upon demand of the loser would make little sense. Where would it take place? If the judge who presided agreed that error had been committed he could grant a new trial and conduct it in such a way as to avoid the mistake the second time through. But if he considered the first trial properly conducted in every respect and the result right, what would be the point in going through the same performance again before him or one of his peers?

Because no satisfactory answer can be given to such questions, a different type of review is provided. It consists of the scrutiny of the record of the original trial by a group of judges bent on discovering whether any error was committed that would vitiate the result. If such an error is found the judgment must be upset. If not, it stands. Not all errors are subject to successful challenge on appeal. Those committed by the jury (if there was one) are constitutionally insulated against review except insofar as they may have been caused or permitted by erroneous rulings of the judge, for instance, if he failed to direct a verdict in a crystal-clear case. Ordinarily only the errors of the judge are open to appellate scrutiny, and furthermore, before the appellate court can order a reversal it must be satisfied that whatever error is found was prejudicial, thus affecting the final judgment. This means that if the judge made an erroneous ruling in excluding a piece of evidence but then in effect canceled it by a subsequent ruling admitting the same evidence when offered later the error would be considered harmless and disregarded. Finally, an appellate court will not interfere in areas of acknowledged trial court discretion, like sentencing in criminal cases. If a sentence is illegal it will be set right, but if it is merely excessive, though within legal limits, it will in most states not warrant appellate court interference.

An appellate court is vastly different from a trial court. Instead of a single judge there are several—at least three, sometimes five or seven or nine. There is no jury. No witnesses are heard or evidence taken. Even the parties themselves are rarely present, for this is a proceeding that the lawyers and judges can perfectly well manage alone.

Beyond the value of saving time and concentrating attention upon the critically important steps of the trial where mistakes are claimed to have been made, there is another value in this type of review, not present in trial *de novo*. This is uniformity in the interpretation of the law. With one central appellate court a statute or rule can have only one meaning in all the trial courts. Uniformity is accomplished in part by direct action upon the judgments of the various trial courts throughout the state; in part, it is accomplished by opinions handed down by the appellate court in the course of reaching its decisions. Decisions, as we shall see in greater detail in Part Two, become guide lines for the future, binding all lower courts that are confronted by substantially similar cases.

The Record on Appeal

Since the object of an appeal is to discover and appraise errors that may have been committed in the trial court, the record of proceedings there becomes a matter of prime importance. The record consists of a stenographic transcript of the testimony taken in the court below, the formal papers used there (pleadings, and so forth), and the verdict and judgment. These papers, or relevant excerpts from them—depending upon the questions to be argued on the appeal—are printed or otherwise duplicated to allow one copy for each of the judges in the appellate court. The job of preparing the papers and submitting them to the clerk of the appellate court for distribtuion to the judges normally falls on the *appellant*, the party who, having lost below, is taking the appeal.

The legal fees involved in taking an appeal and the mechanical costs of preparing the necessary papers pose a serious problem for the indigent litigant. It is partially solved, however, by a combination of devices designed to put him, as nearly as possible, on a par with a man of means. One is that permission is given him to appeal *in forma pauperis*, meaning, as a practical matter, that he is allowed to dispense with the printing of the appeal papers. Another, applicable only in criminal cases however, is furnishing him with a free copy of the stenographic transcript of his trial.[4] Finally and most important, the indigent defendant in a serious criminal case is required to be provided with counsel free of charge for the taking of his appeal. This requirement is the result of a 1963 decision of the Supreme Court of the United States.

Use of Briefs

Along with the record, each judge receives *briefs,* or written arguments, from both sides. The one submitted on behalf of the appellant points out the errors claimed to exist and argues that they are of such a nature as to require reversal of the judgment. The brief of the *appellee,* or *respondent,* the winner below, who is trying to save the judgment, is defensive, arguing that the rulings objected to by the other side are not errors, or, if they are, that they are not sufficiently serious to warrant upsetting the judgment. Both sides cite authorities in the form of statutes and previous cases thought to justify their positions. Though arbitrary limitations on length are imposed by some courts, each brief is likely to run to fifty, sixty, or more printed pages, with the consequence that substantial printing or duplicating expenses may be involved. Sometimes the appellant files a reply brief in rebuttal of the respondent's argument. The briefs are exchanged between the lawyers (the appellant's is due first, then the appellee's, then the reply brief, if any) and filed in court in advance of the time for oral argument. The process ordinarily requires several months after the judgment in the court below.

Oral Argument

With written arguments available for study by the judges, one may wonder why there is need for oral argument as well. One or the other would seem to be enough. Such is the philosophy in England where there are no written briefs and where oral arguments are of unlimited duration, often lasting several days, sometimes even weeks.

In the United States the judges want both types of argument, although most of them tend to rely more on the briefs and to limit oral argument. In the Supreme Court each side ordinarily is allowed one hour; in many other courts considerably less time is allowed—sometimes no more than fifteen or thirty minutes for each side. Part of the time may be consumed by questioning from the judges, but this practice depends upon the mental habits and personalities of the judges and upon whether they make it a practice to study the briefs in advance. Rarely is any time spent reading to the court from the record, the briefs, or the legal authorities relied upon. Most judges object to counsel reading anything aloud, preferring to read for themselves at their own pace and in the privacy of their chambers. What they chiefly want from oral argument is a quick understanding of the case presented to them for decision, with a clear delineation of the issues and the principal lines of reasoning relied on by both sides.

The judges do not attempt to reach a conclusion immediately upon the close of argument. Almost invariably, they reserve judgment until they have had time to study the papers and to carefully formulate a decision. Arguments are heard in groups, several cases being scheduled each day over a period of a week or two. Then the judges adjourn for two or three weeks for the preparation of opinions. Several weeks or months may elapse between oral argument and decision in a given case. In this respect again, American practice differs sharply from English. There, the judges hear one case at a time and customarily deliver their opinions orally and extemporaneously immediately upon completion of oral argument.

Appellate Opinions

Reaching a correct decision is not considered the full discharge of an American appellate court's responsibility. The court is also expected to explain its reasons in writing. Partly this is to satisfy the disappointed litigants that their contentions have been carefully considered. Partly it is to improve the decisional process itself by forcing the judges into the discipline of written explanations and away from snap judgments. Partly it is to clarify and mold the law, for each decision becomes a precedent, governing like cases that may arise in the future.

After a group of cases has been argued, the judges customarily hold a private conference to reach tentative agreement as to decisions to be rendered. Views expressed and votes cast at this time are understood to be subject to later revision. Then, for each case, one of the judges assumes the responsibility of drafting an opinion for court. His selection may be pursuant to a prearranged system of rotating cases between the judges in numerical sequence or by special assignment of the presiding judge, depending upon the custom of the particular court. It is not the custom for each judge to prepare his own opinion. Rather, the ideal is a single opinion representing the view of the entire court, or, failing that, one which represents the view of a majority of the judges, possibly accompanied by a dissenting or concurring opinion for the judges in the minority. Occasionally there is an even greater fragmentation of viewpoints necessitating several dissenting and concurring opinions, but this is rare.

The judge to whom an opinion is assigned first studies the record and the briefs, sometimes supplementing such study by independent research into the law, and then drafts an opinion that he hopes will meet the approval of his colleagues. He circulates his opinion among them for criticisms and suggestions. Further conferences and interchanges of memoranda may ensue, formal or informal, until all of the judges who have to be satisfied (the whole court, the majority, or the minority) are content. The final language of the opinion may be the result of many compromises and not correspond to that which would have been used by any one of the judges writing independently. Furthermore, sometimes what started out to be a minority viewpoint may come to represent the view of the majority or even the entire court. The judges feel free to change their minds at any time until their decision is publicly announced. While each has the responsibility of drafting opinions in the cases assigned to him, he also has the responsibility of studying the cases assigned to his colleagues and the opinions drafted by them. The decision in every case is intended to be the composite result of the deliberations of all the judges.

Publication of Opinions

If appellate opinions are to serve their intended purpose as precedents, they must be available to the bench and bar for guidance. The simple solution is to publish them. This is done on a massive scale in the United States, where hundreds of volumes of opinions are printed each year, some officially, some privately. In general, no attempt is made to separate wheat from chaff, and all opinions of all appellate courts are published without discrimination. Here again is a sharp contrast with the practice in England, where only selected opinions—those which enunciate new principles of law—are published. In the United States important opinions enunciating new legal principles tend to become buried among the hundreds that do nothing more than apply well-settled ones to particular fact patterns.

There are advantages as well as disadvantages in the American approach. On the positive side is the fact that the vast accumulation of judicial rulings upon concrete situations makes the law highly specific and limits the discretion that judges would otherwise exercise if they were guided by nothing but a set of broad, general principles. On the negative side is the complexity of the law resulting from treating as precedents a wilderness of single instances. Citations in briefs are multiplied to an unreasonable extent until one can scarcely see the forest for the trees. The work of judges and lawyers is increased and so is the expense to clients. More books are needed to find the relevant cases—more indexes, digests, texts, encyclopedias—and we can even see beginnings of the need for electronic data retrieval machines to cope with the increasingly unmanageable bulk of our law.

Further Review

The procedure described above applies not only to state supreme courts, but also to intermediate appellate courts where those bodies exist. In some states, therefore, double appellate review becomes possible, and indeed necessary to resolve differences of opinion that inevitably arise between the intermediate courts. Some cases may be allowed to go up as a matter of right (such as those involving an interpretation of the state constitution), but most cases are allowed further review only in the discretion of the state supreme court, which chooses between those offered upon the basis of their importance.

Within the federal judicial system are found intermediate appellate courts also. These are the eleven United States courts of appeals to which the judgments of the ninety-one federal district courts can be appealed as a matter of right.

Unique Position of the Supreme Court

At the summit of appellate tribunals is the Supreme Court of the United States. It has power to review not only decisions of the lower federal courts but also decisions of the highest courts of the various states. While it decides only about 125 appeals a year, the cases are likely to be of great significance.

Almost all cases that reach the Court have already been through at least one stage of appellate review, either in one of the fifty state supreme courts or one of the eleven federal courts of appeals. A few, however, come directly from trial courts. In some special situations (for example, where an act of Congress has been held unconstitutional), a direct appeal may be taken from a United States district court. Similarly, direct review of the decision of a lower state court is possible in exceptional circumstances. In 1960 a case of this kind arose. A man was convicted of loitering and disorderly conduct in a police court of Louisville, Kentucky, and fined $10. He claimed that the proceedings violated the due process clause of the Fourteenth Amendment, but under the statutes there was no higher state court to which he could appeal in so seemingly trivial a case. In these circumstances the Supreme Court of the United States granted review of the case and reversed the conviction. Such situations are exceedingly rare.[5]

A state case can reach the Court only if it involves a question of federal law of controlling importance. State courts are required to apply federal law wherever it is applicable, but since the scope of such law is limited relatively few of their cases are affected by it. Most state cases involve torts, contracts, real property, and other areas of private law where there is no federal legislation and where, moreover, no federal constitutional question is raised. With such cases the Supreme Court has no concern, for it acknowledges that state courts have the final word on questions of state law.

In a relatively small proportion of state cases, federal questions are present, which may or may not be controlling. Thus a litigant might challenge a state statute as being in conflict with both the state constitution and the federal Constitution. If the highest court of the state invalidated the statute on the ground that it violated the state constitution or on the ground that it violated both constitutions the Supreme Court of the United States would have no interest in the case. The state ground of decision would be adequate to support it, and the federal question would have become moot. If, on the other hand, the state court upheld the statute under the state constitution but invalidated it under the federal Constitution the case would be appropriate for review in the Supreme Court.

The federal ground of decision, in other words, would be controlling. Similarly if a claim predicated upon a federal statute (like the Federal Employers' Liability Act) were brought in a state court and if the highest state appellate court interpreted the statute in such a way as to bar the claim, and if that were the sole basis for its decision, the case would present an appropriate question for review in the Supreme Court of the United States.

Insofar as its cases come from the lower federal courts, the Supreme Court again is a specialized tribunal, concentrating on the same kinds of questions. Potentially all cases in federal courts are eligible for ultimate review in the Supreme Court, regardless of the questions litigated. Nevertheless, the jurisdiction of these courts is such as to ensure that the only questions they yield for review are federal questions. The only criminal cases they handle are those involving violations of the federal criminal statutes; and about half of their civil cases arise under the Constitution, laws or treaties of the United States. It is only in the remaining half of the civil cases—those based solely upon diversity of citizenship—that nonfederal questions might be expected to develop. Insofar as such cases involve incidentally questions of federal law (the constitutional right to trial by jury, for example), they are on a par with the cases already discussed. Insofar as they involve questions of state law, such questions are important to decision in the lower federal courts, but they are of little concern to the Supreme Court. There is no dispute as to the general proposition that on such questions state decisions and state statutes are controlling, so that the only problem for the Supreme Court is to see that the lower federal courts respect state sources of decision.

Today relatively few cases reach the Supreme Court as a matter of right. At one time many did, but the press of business was such that Congress gave the Court a very large measure of control over its own docket. The objective was to allow it to concentrate its energies on crucial questions of nationwide concern. Today, as a consequence, most cases reach the Court only by its permission. A litigant seeking review serves on the other parties and files with the court a *petition for certiorari*, in which he seeks not so much to show that an error was committed below as to demonstrate that the question presented is one of general interest, deserving consideration by the highest tribunal of the land. The Court grants or denies review on the basis of its estimate of the importance of the case, measured not in terms of money or penalties but in terms of national significance. Less than 10 percent of the cases that seek review are accepted by the Court.

The few cases that do reach the Court as a matter of right are called *appeals,* and they lie in the following circumstances:

> From a United States court of appeals if a party is relying on a state statute held to be invalid "as repugnant to the Constitution, treaties or laws of the United States."

> From a state court if its decision is against the validity of a treaty or statute of the United States; or if it upholds a state statute against the contention that it is "repugnant to the Constitution, treaties or laws of the United States."

The difficulties of arriving at decision are great in the Supreme Court because of the large number of judges whose views must be consulted (nine judges as against five or seven in most appellate courts) and because of the nature of the questions presented, involving, as they do, profound questions of national policy. In the Supreme Court, the law-giving function of appellate review assumes greater importance than the function of ensuring correct decisions in individual cases. Its emphasis is exactly the reverse of that found in trial *de novo* where reaching the correct result is all that counts. The two types of review are at opposite poles, though both are important and both serve useful purposes.

Chapter Eight

Relations of the Judiciary to Other Branches of Government

The three branches of government are often described as equal, coordinate, and independent, but this generalization needs to be qualified. To some extent the courts control the legislative and executive branches of government; and to some extent those branches control the courts. The interactions between them are the subject of this chapter. We shall first consider the control exercised *by* the courts, and then the control exercised *over* them.

Judicial Powers

CONSTITUTIONALITY OF STATUTES The most dramatic assertion of judicial power occurs when a court holds invalid the act of a duly constituted legislative body. The power of courts to declare statutes unconstitutional was intimated in a limited sense in the supremacy clause of the United States Constitution:

> This Constitution, and the Laws of the United States which shall be made in Pursuance thereof; and all Treaties made, or

which shall be made, under the Authority of the United States, shall be the supreme Law of the Land; and the Judges in every State shall be bound thereby, any Thing in the Constitution or Laws of any State to the Contrary notwithstanding.

The power was not fully and firmly established, however, until 1803 in the famous case of *Marbury v. Madison.*[6] Chief Justice John Marshall said, speaking of an act of Congress:

> The powers of the legislature are defined and limited; and that those limits may not be mistaken, or forgotten, the Constitution is written. To what purpose are powers limited, and to what purpose is that limitation committed to writing, if these limits may, at any time, be passed by those intended to be restrained? The distinction between a government with limited and unlimited powers is abolished, if those limits do not confine the persons on whom they are imposed, and if acts prohibited and acts allowed, are of equal obligation. It is a proposition too plain to be contested, that the Constitution controls any legislative act repugnant to it. . . .
>
> It is emphatically the province and duty of the judicial department to say what the law is. Those who apply the rule to particular cases, must of necessity expound and interpret that rule. If two laws conflict with each other, the courts must decide on the operation of each.

The idea that a court may strike down a legislative enactment has now grown familiar to Americans but it was a bold innovation when first announced; and in many other nations it is still regarded as a radical conception. In England, for example, the courts do not presume to exercise any such power, for the English Parliament is conceded to be supreme, and no written constitution stands in its way. Even in some of the nations that have written constitutions, legislative supremacy rather than judicial supremacy is the rule. Rights spelled out by the constitution of such a nation need be heeded only to the extent that the legislature sees fit. That body, rather than any court, acts as the guardian and interpreter of the constitution.

The Supreme Court of the United States, though the most prominent, is not the only court concerned with constitutional litigation. The lower federal courts and the state courts are also called upon to decide the constitutionality of acts of Congress and of state statutes. An act of Congress may be challenged as being outside the area of legislative power entrusted to the central government or as violating an individual right guaranteed by the United States Constitution. If so challenged, the state or federal court where the question is raised must decide it, subject to ultimate review in the Supreme Court of the United States. Similarly, a state statute may be challenged as invading the powers of the central government or as violating an individual right guaranteed either by the federal or the state constitution or both. If so, again the state or federal court where the question is raised must decide it. Insofar as the question involves only an interpretation of the state constitution, the state supreme court has the final word. Insofar as the United States Constitution is involved, the Supreme Court of the United States has the final word.

Constitutional questions can be and frequently are raised in ordinary litigation of the type described in chapters Two through Six. Thus a man being criminally prosecuted under a statute that he considers unconstitutional may resist conviction upon that ground, and the trial court is forced to consider and decide the question, subject, of course, to appellate review. Or a person engaged in civil litigation may challenge as unconstitutional a statute invoked against him and seek judgment in his favor upon that ground. Again the trial court must decide the constitutional question, and again its decision is subject to appellate review.

Sometimes a suit is brought for the sole and express purpose of having a legislative enactment declared unconstitutional. Such was the 1962 case of *Baker v. Carr*, where citizens of certain counties in Tennessee claimed that their voting rights were greatly diluted by the failure of the state legislature since 1901 to reapportion the state in accordance with population changes that had taken place since then. Claiming that they were denied equal protection of the law under the Fourteenth Amendment to the United States Constitution, they sought, in a federal district court, a declaration of their rights and an injunction preventing state officials from conducting further elections under the old statute. When the case reached the Supreme Court, it held that the question was an appropriate one for it to decide (it had been argued that it was a political rather than a judicial question, as indeed it would have been in almost any other nation in the world), and that if the voters were able to prove their claims upon trial they would be entitled to relief.[7]

Executive action that violates constitutional rights can be challenged in the same way as legislation. In a recent case, the parents of ten New York school children objected to the recitation of the following prayer in classrooms at the beginning of each day:

> Almighty God, we acknowledge our dependence upon Thee, and we beg Thy blessings upon us, our parents, our teachers and our Country.

The prayer had been composed by the state Board of Regents and adopted by the local school board, although no pupil was compelled to take part. Any child could be excused from the room during the recitation upon written request of his parent, and if not so excused, was "free to stand or not stand, to recite or not recite, without fear of reprisal or even comment by the teacher or any school official." The parents brought action in a New York state court to compel the school board to discontinue use of the prayer, claiming that it violated the right of themselves and their children to freedom of religion guaranteed by the Fourteenth Amendment to the United States Constitution. The state trial court and two appellate courts in the state found no substance in their claim, but the Supreme Court of the United States reversed, upholding the contentions of the parents.[8]

It goes without saying that a court cannot invalidate a statute or an executive action merely because of dislike of it or doubt of its wisdom. The ground must be that it conflicts with the United States Constitution or a valid federal law passed pursuant to it, or with the state constitution. Whether the distinction is a substantial one we shall leave to be debated in courses on constitutional law.

REVIEW OF ADMINISTRATIVE DECISIONS In addition to courts, many administrative tribunals are in operation throughout the United States doing much the same kind of work as the courts and in substantially similar fashion.

Familiar examples are the workmen's compensation boards found in almost every state. They handle claims against employers and their insurance companies arising out of personal injuries sustained by their employees at work. Until about half a century ago such claims were litigated in the regular courts, where they accounted for a large share of the total judicial business. Then the public became dissatisfied and inaugurated sweeping changes. No longer was recovery to depend upon fault of the employer and absence of fault by the employee; nor was an employee to be denied recovery because he had assumed the risk of injury or because of the negligence of a fellow employee. Henceforth the sole question would be whether the injury arose out of and in the course of employment. If so, the injured man was entitled to compensation. Furthermore, changes were made in the methods of computing and paying benefits, and a fixed schedule of benefits was established. Instead of having a jury make a single award to cover such unmeasurable items as pain and suffering and loss of future earnings, payments were to be made according to a fixed schedule of benefits—so much for an arm, so much for loss of the sight of an eye, and so forth —and, insofar as loss of earnings was involved, payments were to be made weekly or monthly, spread over the period of disability. Finally, administration of the program was entrusted to specially created administrative agencies—which did not fit neatly into any of the three traditional branches of government. With the legislative functions that some such agencies have in making rules for the better guarding of machinery and general industrial safety, or their executive functions in enforcing such rules, we are not presently concerned; but we are concerned with their judicial functions. They are not called *courts* and those who decide their cases are not called *judges,* but their work is fundamentally similar. When a claim for compensation is contested, they must determine the nature and extent of the injuries suffered and whether they arose out of and in the course of employment— problems not much different from those faced by courts in passing upon claims of injured railroad workers arising under the Federal Employers Liability Act. Their procedures are different—for there are no formal pleadings, no technical rules of evidence, no juries—but their functions are much the same as those of courts in receiving and evaluating evidence and in applying the law to the facts so found.

Other administrative tribunals handle other problems —some of the type just considered, which were formerly handled by the courts, and others like minimum wage claims or veterans' benefits, which upon their first appearance were entrusted to administrative tribunals. The list of such problems is still growing; and today there is much serious talk of devising a system for the handling of personal injury claims arising out of automobile accidents which would be modeled upon the workmen's compensation plans.

Whatever the nature of these tribunals or their jurisdiction their decisions are subject to review in the courts. Those agencies operating under the authority of the state government come under the control of the courts of that state, whereas those operating under the authority of the federal government come under the control of the federal courts. Sometimes initial review is by a trial court and sometimes by an appellate court, but in either case the court exercises an appellate function. It does not hear the evidence again, but reviews the record of proceedings in the administrative tribunal to determine whether there is any evidence to support the conclusion and whether the governing law has been correctly interpreted and applied. Because of real or imagined specialization and *expertise* in administrative tribunals, their decisions are seldom upset by the courts. But the fact they can be and occasionally are upset is one of the measures of judicial control over other agencies of government.

HABEAS CORPUS AND OTHER EXTRAORDINARY REMEDIES Habeas corpus is one of several procedures developed by the English courts centuries ago to control officers of the executive branch of the government. Its primary (but not sole) use was to compel jailers to produce persons in their custody before a court that could inquire into the cause of their detention. If no legal justification for detention could be shown, the prisoner was released. Today, that purpose is accomplished largely by the preliminary hearing before a magistrate described in Chapter Three. In exceptional situations, however, where an ordinary preliminary hearing would not be appropriate, habeas corpus is still available. It was recently used in England, for example, in the Soblen spy case. After Soblen's appeal from his conviction for treason in an American court had failed, he fled to Israel. He was deported, and while returning to the United States by plane to serve his sentence (there was a United States marshal aboard), he stabbed himself in the abdomen. The plane put down in England, where Soblen was placed in a prison hospital. His English lawyers secured a writ of habeas corpus to inquire into the legality of his detention but the final decision was against him.

In England, habeas corpus has never been used to review convictions by courts having jurisdiction over the offender and the crime. Such review is possible only by way of appeal. In the United States, however, a curious development has been taking place in recent years. A theory has evolved to the effect that if a court trying a criminal case violates a constitutional right of the accused it is thereby ousted of jurisdiction. This stretches the meaning of traditional concepts and procedures almost beyond the point of recognition and allows habeas corpus to be used as a virtual substitute for appeal. Hence we see the strange spectacle of a conviction in a state court being reviewed on habeas corpus in a federal district court, sometimes after the conviction has been affirmed on appeal by the highest court of the state, with certiorari denied by the Supreme Court of the United States! In this situation, of course, the writ is not being used for its original and primary purpose of controlling executive action but as a procedure whereby one court reviews the rulings of another court (the latter sometimes superior in status to the reviewing court).

Other procedures developed by the early English courts to control executive action include: (1) *mandamus* ("we command"), which is used to compel an official to perform a routine act that, though legally obliged to perform, he refuses to do (like registering a motor vehicle or issuing a marriage license); (2) *prohibition*, which is used to prevent an official body exercising quasi-judicial functions from acting beyond its powers (for example, a state board of health could be restrained from attempting to disbar a lawyer); and (3) *quo warranto* ("by what authority?"), which is used to prevent someone from usurping an office that does not belong to him (for example, it could be used to oust a person acting as police chief who had not been regularly elected or appointed).

To these *extraordinary remedies*, as they are called, must be added the more familiar remedy of the *injunction*, described briefly in Chapter Five, which is a court order commanding a person to do or refrain from doing a certain act. Since the act in question may be the enforcement of a statute that is invalid or inapplicable, this remedy can be and frequently is used against government officials.

The Role of the Executive Branch

Despite its extensive powers, the judicial branch of government is no more omnipotent than the other branches. It too is subject to checks and balances.

The lifeblood of any institution is the quality of its personnel. This is decidedly true of the courts, for if the judges are competent, honest, impartial, and hard working, they can make almost any system of law work tolerably well; but if they are incompetent, corrupt, biased, or lazy, they can ruin the best of systems. The selection of judges, therefore, becomes a matter of the utmost importance; and here the role of the executive branch of the government looms large.

In the federal government and in a few states, judges are appointed by the chief executive, though sometimes subject to legislative approval and sometimes subject to a preliminary screening of candidates by a nominating commission. In a majority of the states judges are popularly elected, but even in such states the governor has the power to make temporary appointments to fill vacancies when judges die, resign, or retire before the expiration of their terms. Many, if not most, men initially go on the bench as a result of such temporary appointments, and then as sitting judges are elected to full terms.

The fact that many judges are appointed, at least initially, and often for reasons that are in large part political, does not mean that their decisions are controlled by the appointing authority. Nowhere is this more clearly shown than in the history of the Supreme Court, whose justices have, as often as not, refused to follow the political views of the Presidents who appointed them. The independence of judges is reinforced by their tenure, which is sometimes for life "during good behavior," sometimes for a specified period of time. They cannot be removed at the will of either the appointing power or the legislature. True, they can be *impeached*—meaning legislatively tried and removed for misconduct, or, in some states, eliminated from office by a special court on the judiciary (usually composed of senior judges)—but at least they are well insulated from anything resembling direct control over their decisions.

The only other way in which the executive branch of government might affect the functioning of the courts would be by withholding enforcement of their judgments, some of which are unpopular in the extreme, and some of which are directed against the executive branch of the government itself. The courts themselves have no machinery for enforcement. Ordinarily none is needed, for voluntary compliance, however reluctant, is usually forthcoming; but in some situations, as in the violent storm caused by the Supreme Court's School Segregation decision,[9] strong-arm methods of enforcement are necessary, occasionally even the use of the armed forces.

With very rare exceptions such support has been given when needed by the executive branch. Indeed, on several occasions Presidents and governors have accepted and enforced judicial decisions that were highly distasteful to them. The withdrawal of such executive support would render the courts impotent.

The Role of the Legislative Branch

Legislative power over the courts is more extensive and more vital than executive power. It extends to virtually every facet of their operations, as the following catalogue will demonstrate.

COURT STRUCTURE AND ADMINISTRATION   Except to the extent that the organization, jurisdiction, and administration of the courts are defined constitutionally, legislatures have power to say which courts shall exist, how they shall be organized, and what cases they shall handle. In the federal system, for example, Congress could abolish the lower federal courts entirely or drastically curtail their jurisdiction, as by depriving them of their power over diversity of citizenship cases. It could take away from the Supreme Court its appellate jurisdiction over habeas corpus proceedings or any other class of cases. It could and did establish the Administrative Office of the United States Courts and the Judicial Conference of the United States, the two agencies that bring unity and centralization of administration into the system. By exercise of the same power, Congress could abolish them, leaving the individual courts as isolated, autonomous, and unsupervised as they were before, held together only by the thin threads of appellate review.

State legislatures possess similar powers. Within whatever constitutional limitations that may exist they can create unified systems of courts with full-time professional judges and centralized administration, or they can allow to develop or continue a motley conglomeration of disparate and disorganized units, some of them manned by part-time lay justices of the peace.

NUMBER OF JUDGES Constitutional provisions ordinarily do not fix the number of judges, but leave that to legislative control. Again the situation in the federal courts is instructive. While the Supreme Court is established by the Constitution, the number of its judges is not fixed in that document, thus it has varied from five to ten. In the middle 1930s, the Supreme Court was invalidating much of the New Deal legislative program, and President Franklin D. Roosevelt conceived the idea of "packing" the court. This was to be accomplished by Congress increasing the number of judges and the President filling the new offices with men more sympathetic to the New Deal. The court-packing plan failed in Congress after a bitter fight. But the views of the Supreme Court changed at almost the same time, so that most New Deal legislation survived.

What is true of legislative power over the number of

judges on the highest court is also generally true with respect
to the number in the lower courts, federal and state. In
1960, Congress added about 100 new judges to the United
States district courts and the courts of appeal, not for any
ulterior purpose, but to enable them to cope with an increasing caseload and to bring their dockets up to date. State
legislatures also, from time to time, have increased the number of their judges. Where justice is too long delayed the
fault may not be so much with the judges as with the legislative bodies that have neglected to augment their number.

SELECTION OF JUDGES   In a few states, the legislatures
appoint the judges. In a few others, and in the federal government, they have the power of veto over executive appointments. Some legislative bodies also have indirect power to
control the quality of the judges by prescribing their qualifications (specifying, for example, whether they must be lawyers)
and determining the method of their selection.

In a majority of states, as already noted, the judges are
popularly elected, and in some of these states judges run for
office on partisan political ballots. Many persons are persuaded that this is the wrong way to pick judges because the
voters seldom know or care for whom they vote, being content
to leave that to the political bosses. Such persons favor either
the appointive system or another method of selection which
has come to be variously known as the "American Bar Asso-
ciation Plan" or the "American Judicature Society Plan" or
the "Missouri Plan." In essence, it provides for the creation of
an impartial, nonpartisan nominating commission whose job
it is to submit to the governor a list of names of persons
eligible for appointment. The governor makes his selection
from the list and appoints the man for a limited time. At the
end of that time, and at the expiration of each term, the
judge runs for election against his own record, not against
any other candidate. The question presented to the voters is
simply whether or not the judge should be retained in office.

The plan has worked well in the states where it has been tried. It tends to make judicial tenure more stable, and to minimize (though not completely to eliminate) the influence of partisan politics in the selection process. Partisan politics, of course, is a prime evil in both the pure elective and the pure appointive systems. Where a state constitution does not itself prescribe the method of selecting judges, the legislature possesses the power to inaugurate this or any other improved plan.

JUDICIAL SALARIES, TENURE, AND RETIREMENT

The salaries of judges are legislatively controlled. The more generous they are, within limits, the more likely they are to attract able lawyers and so improve the functioning of the judicial system. Here is an area where legislative leadership can be significant. Disparities in salaries over the nation are striking. Federal district court judges receive $22,500 per year, court of appeals judges $25,500, and Supreme Court justices $35,000—the Chief Justice receiving an additional $500. From these figures there are wide variations in both directions. In Kansas a judge of the trial court of general jurisdiction receives $12,000 per year while his counterpart in New York City receives $34,500 per year. Both are on a par functionally with the federal district court judges sitting in their own states.

Tenure presents a somewhat different problem, for in some states and in the federal government, it is fixed constitutionally. Where this is not so, the legislature can act. Quite obviously, the attractiveness of a judicial post carrying life tenure "during good behavior" (the term of office in the federal courts and those of a few states) is greater than that of one which carries tenure for only a few years (only a two-year term in Vermont).

Retirement plans also affect the attractiveness of judicial posts, and they too are subject to legislative control. Plans vary from the federal system where a judge can receive full pay for life upon retirement at age seventy after serving ten years or at age sixty-five after serving fifteen years to systems so inadequate that judges are almost forced to stay on the bench long after their powers have failed.

NONJUDICIAL PERSONNEL AND COURT FACILI-TIES   Courts are composed not only of judges but also of a far greater number of additional persons who assist the judges in their work, such as law clerks in the appellate courts and social workers and probation officers in criminal, juvenile, and family courts. Unless the legislature provides money for their employment, their services are not available and the work of the courts is affected correspondingly.

   Physical facilities also affect the judicial process. Many courtrooms, especially those of the minor courts that are most often entered by great masses of the population and which, therefore, tend to fix the public image of justice, are un-dignified, unattractive, and lacking in proper accommodations for jurors, witnesses, litigants, lawyers, and sometimes even judges. Auxiliary facilities are often similarly inadequate. Some criminals are not prosecuted because the jails are not big enough to hold them; others are put on probation for the same reason; and still others are released from prison because the space they occupy is needed for new inmates. This inadequacy is also true of prison hospitals, reform schools, and work camps.

   Such problems cannot be solved without money, and legislatures hold the purse strings.

PROCEDURAL RULE-MAKING   In some states the rules by which courts operate are made by the legislature. In others and in the federal government, that power has been delegated in large measure to the courts themselves on the theory that courts understand such problems better and are more responsive to changing needs. Representative of statutes so delegating rule-making power was an act of Congress, passed in 1934, giving the Supreme Court of the United States the power to prescribe rules of procedure for the federal district courts. The rules were not to abridge, enlarge, or modify the substantive rights of any litigant or the constitutional right to trial by jury. They were to be reported to Congress (in time for it to make changes) and then to take effect, superseding all laws in conflict with them.

The Supreme Court, acting under this statute, appointed an advisory committee composed of distinguished judges, lawyers, and law professors, which, in turn, appointed a staff to do the job of draftsmanship. Successive drafts were prepared and submitted to the entire profession for comments and suggestions, and, in 1938, a set of modern, simple rules was adopted by the Supreme Court. They have been amended several times since then, following substantially the same procedure as that originally used. So successful have the rules been in minimizing technicalities and in securing the just, speedy, and inexpensive determination of cases on the merits that they have been widely acclaimed and copied throughout the nation. About half the states now have rules modeled very largely upon the federal pattern. In the field of criminal procedure, too, the Supreme Court was granted rule-making power, and its rules, promulgated in 1944, are also generally regarded as models for state reform.

In granting rule-making power to the Supreme Court, Congress reserved veto power in itself, thus maintaining ultimate legislative control over procedure. Similar provisions can be found in the statutes of about half of the states.

SUBSTANTIVE LAW   No legislative body has power to reverse a judicial decision. Unless the decision is based upon a constitutional ground, however, a legislature may cancel its effect as a precedent by enacting a contrary rule. Hundreds of examples can be cited of alterations in judge-made law effectuated by legislation. Much more unusual is the obliteration of a precedent by a constitutional amendment, as recently happened in Arizona. In 1962, the supreme court of that state ruled that real estate brokers were engaging in the unauthorized practice of law when they drafted leases or deeds to property for their customers. The realtors, not content with seeking a mere legislative change in the rule, obtained enough signatures on an initiative petition to place the question before the electorate in the form of a proposed constitutional amendment. In November of 1962, it passed by a margin of about four to one in the following form (Article XXVI):

> Any person holding a valid license as a real estate broker or a real estate salesman regularly issued by the Arizona State Real Estate Department when acting in such capacity as broker or salesman for the parties, or agent for one of the parties to a sale, exchange or trade, or the renting and leasing of property, shall have the right to draft or fill out and complete, without charge, any and all instruments, incident thereto including, but not limited to, preliminary purchase agreements and earnest money receipts, deeds, mortgages, leases, assignments, releases, contracts for sale of realty, and bills of sale.

This seems to finally settle the question, but it must be pointed out that the constitutional provision still has to be interpreted by the courts of the state. Can realtors not only draft legal instruments but also advise their customers which ones to sign? Are they now subject to the same ethical rules that govern lawyers? Can they advertise their services as draftsmen of legal instruments? Are they subject to actions for legal malpractice when they make mistakes? These questions, which have already been pointed out by the chief justice of the state, are still to be resolved.

CONSTITUTIONAL CHANGES   As already indicated, some features of the judicial system in each state and in the federal government are fixed by constitutional provisions, not subject to alteration by ordinary statutes. That does not mean, however, that the legislature is powerless to stimulate change. It can prepare whatever constitutional amendments are needed for submission to the voters. These may relate to any of the problems we have discussed: changes in substantive law; the allocation of procedural rule-making powers; the structure, organization, jurisdiction, and administration of the courts; the selection and tenure of judges. Most major reforms in the judicial branch of government have come about in this way, and in almost every case the legislature has led the way.

The Process

of

Decision-making

Introductory Note

The heart of any lawsuit is the psychological process of reaching a decision, a fact seldom acknowledged and even more rarely explained.

Lawyers and judges are prone to talk as if rules rather than people decided cases. As a result, some peculiar and contradictory notions are in circulation. One is that issues of fact (which, in some undefined way, are supposed to be different from issues of law) are either (1) too simple to bother about or, (2) beyond the realm of understanding. Another is that justice results from a formula somewhat as follows: facts + law = justice. In this formula human beings have about as much place as in the multiplication table. Such misconceptions obscure the nature of both fact and law.

The cases to be discussed in Part Two will reveal, it is hoped, that decisions in court are not greatly different from those made outside of court; that they concern, for the most part, familiar day-to-day happenings; that they involve the same kind of mental operations as are used in solving problems that arise in business or housekeeping; and that they can be and frequently are made by ordinary citizens without special training—namely, jurors.

Chapter / *Nine*

Who Is
Telling the Truth

Much of the raw material for decision-making is information furnished by witnesses. The trouble is that they may be
mistaken or lying. If so, any decision based upon their statements is likely to be wrong except by sheer accident.

How can one decide whether another person is telling
the truth? At one time, this seemed an insoluble problem,
requiring supernatural help. Maitland, describing English law
before the advent of the jury, reported:

> . . . in old times proof was not an attempt to convince the
> judges; it was an appeal to the supernatural, and very com-
> monly a unilateral act. The common modes of proof are oaths
> and ordeals. It is adjudged, for example, in an action for debt
> that the defendant do prove his assertion that he owes nothing
> by his own oath and the oaths of a certain number of compur-
> gators or oath-helpers. The defendant must then solemnly swear
> that he owes nothing, and his oath-helpers must swear that
> his oath is clean and unperjured. If they safely get through
> this ceremony, punctually repeating the right formula, there
> is an end of the case; the plaintiff, if he is hardy enough to go
> on, can only do so by bringing a new charge, a criminal charge

of perjury against them. They have not come there to convince the court, they have not come there to be examined and cross examined like modern witnesses, they have come there to bring upon themselves the wrath of God if what they say be not true. This process is known in England as 'making one's law'; a litigant who is adjudged to prove his case in this way is said to "wage his law" . . . when he finds security that on a future day he will bring compurgators and perform this solemnity, then when on the appointed day he comes and performs that ceremony with success, he is said to "make his law." . . . An ordeal is still more obviously an appeal to the supernatural; the judgment of God is given; the burning iron spares the innocent, the water rejects the guilty. Or again the court adjudges that there must be trial by battle; the appellor charges the appellee with a crime, the appellee gives him the lie; the demandant's champion swears that he saw the demandant seised of the land, and is ready to prove this by his body; the wit of man is at fault in presence of a flat contradiction; God will show the truth.[10]

Society today has more confidence in human ability to resolve issues of fact, even when witnesses are flatly contradicting each other. Every day juries are called upon to perform that feat, and they perform it reasonably well. But how? To hear some judges and lawyers talk and see them shaking their heads about juries one would think that the mystery is as profound today as it was in the period Maitland described. They understand fairly well how judges think in deciding questions of law (some good books have been written on that subject), but when they come to issues of fact and juries, they throw up their hands as if to say, "This is incomprehensible."

But is it? Some of the very judges and lawyers who express that attitude are highly skilled in conducting trials and leading juries to desired results. Can it be that they do know how juries think, but are unable to articulate their knowledge? Are they like talented artists who are unable to explain how they achieve their results?

We are handicapped in trying to understand how

jurors think. Only the jurors themselves are in a position to know, and they ordinarily don't tell. They probably can't, for few, if any, of them have the inclination to probe into thought processes that are so largely subconscious. If outsiders get overly curious, they are likely to be sharply repulsed. This happened a few years ago when a research team from the University of Chicago placed hidden microphones in a jury room and tried to listen in. Howls of outrage were heard throughout the nation and the experiment was dropped. Jury deliberations, it seems, were regarded as too sacred to be investigated—at least by a method so direct. The veil of mystery was quickly pulled back into place.

The best we can do, therefore, is to try imaginatively and introspectively to reconstruct what goes on in the mind of a juror. A good vehicle for launching our attempt is a famous trial that took place in 1935, which arose out of the kidnapping and murder of the Lindbergh baby.

Facts of the Lindbergh Case

Colonel Charles A. Lindbergh, the first man to cross the Atlantic by airplane in 1927, became a great national hero. When his infant child was kidnapped from his home one evening in March 1932, public excitement reached fever pitch. A ransom of $50,000 was paid, but the child was not returned. Instead, its dead body was found a short time later near the Lindbergh home in a shallow, hastily dug grave.

Two years later some of the ransom money began circulating, and it led to the arrest in September 1934 of Bruno Hauptmann. He was charged with the kidnapping and murder, and his trial took place in New Jersey. In that trial, the jurors had to decide whether Hauptmann was telling the truth. If he was, a verdict of not guilty was unescapable, and Hauptmann would go free. If he was not, the probability was that Hauptmann would be condemned to death. The case, therefore, is a good one in which to seek an answer to a central question involved in deciding any problem of fact —that of determining credibility.

Direct Testimony

Hauptmann took the stand after the prosecution's evidence, mostly circumstantial, had been completed. That evidence, if believed, was sufficient to convict him, for he had been identified as the man who wrote the notes demanding ransom, received the money, spent part of it and still had some left when he was arrested, and who was enjoying sudden and unexplained prosperity, whose tools and lumber had been used to make the ladder employed in the kidnapping, and who was seen in the vicinity of Hopewell, New Jersey, where the Lindberghs lived, near the time when the crime was committed.

After giving a brief account of his life—blameless except for some unidentified offense committed during his youth in Germany and his subsequent illegal entry into the United States—Hauptmann testified that he knew no more about the Lindbergh kidnapping and murder than he had read in the newspapers; that he had nothing whatever to do with it; that he had never in his life been at or anywhere near the Lindbergh residence; and that he did not write the ransom notes or collect the ransom money. On the evening of March 1, 1932, when the crime was being committed, he was calling for his wife at the combination lunchroom and bakery in the Bronx where she worked as a waitress. On the evening of April 2, 1932, when the ransom money was being paid in St. Raymond's Cemetery by "Jafsie" Condon to a man calling himself "John," Hauptmann was at home enjoying a musical evening, playing a mandolin while one of his friends played a guitar.

Hauptmann's recent prosperity, he said, was due to successful speculations on the stock market. He had formed an informal partnership with a man named Isidore Fisch in March or April 1932, for the purpose of such operations and conducting a fur-trading business which was run by Fisch. Hauptmann conducted the stock market operations from his own home.

His connection with Fisch also explained Hauptmann's possession of some of the Lindbergh ransom money. Fisch, on his way to Germany in December 1933, had left with Hauptmann a cardboard box for safekeeping. What it contained except "paper" Fisch did not say and Hauptmann did not inquire. Hauptmann, thinking no more about the matter, put the box in a broom closet in his home where it remained until August 1934. At that time, Hauptmann, looking for a broom, accidentally broke the box and thus saw the currency it contained. The bills were wet from a leak in the ceiling, so Hauptmann dried them off and put them in a basket, which he then attached to the ceiling of his garage.

As for the handwriting specimens used during the trial by experts in an attempt to demonstrate that Hauptmann had written the ransom notes, they were practically beaten out of him by the police, according to Hauptmann's testimony. He was told even which words to misspell (like "singature" instead of "signature") in order to make them correspond with writing in the ransom notes.

Such was the substance of Hauptmann's story told on direct examination in response to questions by his own lawyer. What he said on cross-examination will be brought out in the ensuing discussion of whether his testimony was worthy of belief.

General Analysis

The jurors must have rejected Hauptmann's testimony, for they found him guilty. They reached that conclusion after being cautioned against it unless they were convinced beyond a reasonable doubt. They acted with full knowledge of their awesome responsibility, for they had been warned by the judge: "If you should return a verdict of murder in the first degree and nothing else, the punishment which would be inflicted on that verdict would be death."

Why did the jurors disbelieve Hauptmann? It is not enough to answer that it was because other witnesses had contradicted him, for such an answer would merely rephrase the basic question: What makes one believe or disbelieve any witness? The jurors were not present to see for themselves any of the events related by Hauptmann or any of the other witnesses. Had they possessed personal knowledge, they would not have been allowed to sit on the jury. The only information they had was what they might have gained from newspapers, radio broadcasts, and gossip. However, each juror, during the preliminary questioning to determine his fitness to serve, was able under oath to satisfy the judge and both lawyers that any opinion he received from such sources was casual rather than fixed, and that he would be guided solely by the evidence and the law as laid down by the judge.

Yet whatever vague and separate impressions may have been entertained by individual members of the jury at the beginning of the trial, these impressions were transformed during the course of the trial into a unanimous belief so strong that it overcame all reasonable doubt. By what alchemy was this accomplished? In less-publicized trials, how are jurors transported from a state of total ignorance to an equally strong belief about events none of them have perceived?

If the answer is not to be found in specific knowledge possessed by the jurors before the trial, then it must be sought in generalized knowledge possessed by them. What, then, was the generalized knowledge of the jurors in the Hauptmann trial, and how was it used in reaching the conclusion that Hauptmann lied?

Briefly, the generalized knowledge consisted of the mental residue of the life experiences of the twelve jurors involved. The range of those experiences is suggested by their ages and occupations. Of the eight men on the jury, one was an unemployed bookkeeper, fifty-five years old; another a retired carpenter, aged sixty; another a machinist, aged fifty-five; another a farmer, aged forty; another an insurance salesman, aged forty-two; another an educational supervisor for the Civilian Conservation Corps, aged twenty-eight; another a railroad employee, aged fifty-eight; and another a farmer, aged fifty-four. Four women completed the panel. One of them, thirty-two years of age and married, was a legal stenographer. The other three were housewives, including one woman who was active in civic and welfare activities.

That all of the jurors must have had experience in judging the credibility of others is evident. In dealing with their parents, children, spouses, schoolmates, business associates, colleagues, and friends, they must have made many dozens of determinations about whether other people were telling the truth. Very likely most of the determinations were made at an almost subconscious level, without explicit analysis. Yet there must also have been times when the factors making for credibility or the lack of it were consciously examined and discussed with others. Thus each juror, as a result of his experiences outside of the courtroom, had a collection of ideas about what makes for truthfulness or the lack of it. Those ideas might be right or wrong, but they certainly existed and gave meaning and significance to what went on in the courtroom.

So much for a very general answer. But what specifically did the jurors in the Hauptmann case know about credibility, and how did they use their knowledge?

Interest as a Factor in Credibility

The jurors knew of Hauptmann's interest in the outcome of the trial. No formal evidence was offered on the matter and none was necessary. The jurors knew enough about murder trials in general and about human psychology in general to realize that Hauptmann's life was at stake and that he knew it.

There was no evidence as to how Hauptmann's interest affected his credibility. Yet the jurors must have known that interest often leads men to falsify in their own favor and that the motive to prevaricate varies in proportion to the strength and vitality of the interest. This they could know from introspective memory of their own experiences, when they had told falsehoods trying to save their own skins or advance their own interests, or from observing children lying about broken toys, stolen cookies, and schoolroom pranks.

The jurors must also have realized, however, that interest is not always controlling. Their experience would tell them that people sometimes tell the truth at great cost to themselves, and that sometimes a story favorable to one's own interest is true in spite of its superficially self-serving quality. Nevertheless, in spite of the fact that they were necessarily dealing in averages, tendencies, and probabilities rather than certainties, the jurors must have been aware that interest was a factor that had to be weighed against Hauptmann's testimony. It rendered the jurors skeptical, put them on guard, made them take his story with a grain of salt. Or more accurately, with two grains, for every witness' story would be received initially with some reservation, whether he had an interest or not.

What about the witnesses for the prosecution? Were they enough interested so that their stories should have been suspect?

Their interest was less apparent, if it existed at all. Several were handwriting experts, others were accountants, others experts on wood, others police officials, others mere observers of some small part of the drama. Not one of them was shown to have any stake in the outcome of the case or any motive to see Hauptmann rather than some other person convicted of the crime charged. Their only interest could have been in maintaining consistency with the stories they had told before trial. But what interest did they have in falsifying those stories when originally told? None that is apparent in the evidence.

Colonel Lindbergh also testified. It is likely that he may have had a strong emotional interest in seeing someone convicted, but why pick on Hauptmann? Colonel Lindbergh had identified him before the trial as the man whose voice he heard in the cemetery when the ransom money was passed. But again, what interest did Colonel Lindbergh have in making a false identification in the first place?

"Jafsie" Condon, the go-between who paid the ransom money to the kidnapper, was a key witness. Eccentric and publicity-loving though he may have been, the evidence shows no more motive on his part than on Colonel Lindbergh's for making a false identification.

Since no interest on the part of the witnesses was shown, none probably existed. This would follow from the jurors' knowledge of how trials are conducted and how lawyers find and produce evidence.

From the conclusion that the prosecution witnesses were disinterested, the inference would have been justified that they had no motive to falsify and were telling the truth unless other factors bearing upon credibility (to be discussed) should indicate the contrary. That inference would be based upon pre-existing beliefs of the jurors, founded upon their total life experiences, that people generally speak the truth if they are unbiased and disinterested. It would be tentative and subject to review, but crucial so long as it survived.

Before going on to other aspects of credibility, perhaps it is possible to make a tentative generalization about the decision-making process seen thus far. The pattern seems to be this:

While some of the raw material for making a decision is information furnished by witnesses, the rest is what is already in the mind of the juror. That mass of information and misinformation about human nature and conduct (for it includes false ideas as well as sound ones, hunches and superstitions as well as reliable knowledge) gives meaning and significance to what he sees and hears in the courtroom. Understanding or believing that he understands the characteristics and relationships of general classes of things, people, and events, he attributes them to the particular things, people, and events presented to him. Evidence bears about the same relationship to his pre-existing ideas as the small part of an iceberg visible above water bears to the vastly larger part lying beneath the surface.

Consistency and Veracity

Another clue to whether Hauptmann's testimony was worthy of belief was the fact that the story he told on the witness stand did not always correspond to what he had said before trial. For example, during his direct examination, he denied that he had written on the door jamb of the closet in his home the telephone number and address of Dr. Condon, the man who, as intermediary for Colonel Lindbergh, paid the ransom money. Cross examination established, however, that in extradition proceedings in New York, Hauptmann had admitted that the handwriting was his, and offered the explanation that he was in the habit of scribbling on walls and doors various bits of information that interested him, such as historical facts and matters of general curiosity.

Manifestly both accounts could not be true. The jurors, as persons of normal intelligence and experience, could only conclude that Hauptmann was mistaken or lying in his first account, or in the account given during trial. The fact that he had made a prior statement inconsistent with his testimony at the trial made it more probable that the latter testimony was false than if he had not made such a statement.

In Hauptmann's case, the serious nature of his inconsistency is illuminated by his admissions on the witness stand that he lied in some of his pretrial statements, that he then told the truth "only to a certain extent." If he deliberately lied before, why not again?

Then, too, he was caught in some lies and evasions during the course of the trial. For example, his story about being forced by the police into misspelling "signature" evinced a readiness, if not an eagerness, to dispense with the truth when that seemed convenient. The prosecution's evidence established that that word, which appeared in one of the ransom notes, did not appear in any of the handwriting specimens given by Hauptmann to the police.

Suppose Hauptmann did lie in a few matters. Does that discredit all of his testimony? Not necessarily, for a man who invariably lied would be as rare as one who invariably told the truth. But if a man lies on one occasion—especially a serious one like a police investigation—he is more likely to lie on another occasion than a man who has not so lied previously; and if he is willing to lie on one aspect of a series of related events, he is probably willing to lie on other aspects.

Thus, common ideas on consistency pointed in the same direction as common ideas on interest—against Hauptmann.

Inherent Probability

Hauptmann's story about his financial affairs did not ring true. Crucial parts of it were inherently improbable and out of character. Until the spring of 1932, he and his wife were hard-working, frugal people, and they pooled their earnings. He seemed to keep track in his account books of every penny earned and every penny spent, and revealed himself in bookkeeping entries as a man fascinated and preoccupied with money. The money he and his wife had was invested in the hope of making more—all except for $4000 in cash, which he claimed at the trial he was hiding from his wife in a trunk in their home. That money was neither recorded nor invested, though Hauptmann was fully aware of the existence of banks and their uses, and too well aware for his own good of the existence of the stock market. In fact, so casual was he about the $4000 that in the summer of 1931 he put it in a suitcase which he left with a relative while he and his wife took a trip to the West Coast.

After April 1932 (when the ransom money was paid), Hauptmann stopped working regularly and his wife stopped working entirely in December of that year. The $4000 was invested, but never recorded in Hauptmann's account books or revealed to his wife. Nor did he keep records of substantial amounts of cash that he said were handed to him by Fisch and then invested in the stock market, or of his advances to Fisch, or of the results of the fur-trading operations in which both men were interested. Meanwhile, however, he kept on making careful entries on relatively trivial investments and transactions. Only occasionally would mention be made of any stock market or fur-trading operations, and those that were mentioned fell far short of explaining his prosperity at the time of the trial.

Hauptmann was similarly casual with the cardboard box that Fisch was supposed to have handed him in December 1933. After discovering the currency it contained, he did not bother to count it for a couple of weeks. Then he put the bills in odd places in his garage, not even in the trunk where he had previously kept his private hoard. He did not record the find in his books or invest it in the stock market or deposit it in a bank. He took a few odd bills from time to time for current expenses.

Hauptmann's story about his financial affairs didn't have the ring of truth. It sounded as if he had manufactured it to explain his possession of the ransom money and his prosperity. Could it be that his initial $4000 hoard of cash and the $15,000 shoebox never existed except in Hauptmann's mind? Could it be that his account books were accurate and complete as a history of legitimate assets, but that they deliberately omitted any reference to the ransom money? How could such a frugal, hard-working man, meticulous in his book-keeping and careful in his investing and safeguarding of money suddenly change character so completely as to give up his job, forget to record major financial transactions, and leave cash lying around unguarded and idle?

Such might have been the questions and doubts that assailed the jurors, again because of their previous knowledge of human nature and conduct in general.

Capacity to Observe and Remember

So far in this attempt to re-create imaginatively the impressions made by Hauptmann's testimony, the knowledge of the jurors seems to have been running consistently against Hauptmann. But one thing was in his favor: His opportunity and capacity to observe and remember crucial events. If any single witness possessed the knowledge needed to solve the puzzle presented the jury and the capacity to give direct rather than circumstantial evidence, it was Hauptmann. No witness for the prosecution claimed to have observed the kidnapping of the Lindbergh baby. All testified merely to circumstances from which inferences as to the event could be made. The conditions under which they observed the circumstances reported at the trial were in some instances such that they might easily have been mistaken. For example, Colonel Lindbergh never saw the man who collected the ransom money and heard him speak only two words in St. Raymond's Cemetery, hailing Dr. Condon: "Hey Doctor!" Lindbergh's memory of the sound of those two words was his sole basis for identifying Hauptmann as the man who uttered them. Dr. Condon saw the man and talked to him at some length, but the cemetery was dark and conditions for observation were not ideal. The men who identified Hauptmann as the man they had seen in the vicinity of the Lindbergh residence near the time of the kidnapping were recalling to mind only fleeting glimpses of a stranger. The handwriting experts who testified to their opinion that Hauptmann wrote the ransom notes had not seen him write them. All might have been mistaken.

But not Hauptmann. He knew where he was and what he was doing at the crucial times, whether he had written the ransom notes or collected the ransom money. He could not have been mistaken. One does not fail to notice or remember whether he has participated in a kidnapping—an observation that any member of the jury might have made had he considered something so obvious worthy of mention.

On the score of his ability to observe and remember, then, Hauptmann rated high. By that criterion, his testimony was entitled to greater credence than that of any other witness. But credibility depends upon something more than a witness' ability to tell the truth; it also depends upon his willingness. On that score, Hauptmann rated low.

Contradiction and Corroboration

Helping the jury decide whether to believe Hauptmann because of his superior capacity to observe and remember or to disbelieve him because of his apparent insincerity was the testimony of other witnesses. Hauptmann was corroborated by prosecution witnesses only on the damaging parts of his testimony: his prior statements to the police; the location of ransom bills in his garage; the fact that he quit his job in April 1932 (when the ransom money was paid). The part of his testimony that supported his claim of innocence was contradicted. His claim that he was never near Lindbergh's home was contradicted by three witnesses who testified to having seen him in the vicinity near the time of the crime. Hauptmann's claim that he had not written the ransom notes was contradicted by eight handwriting experts. His claim that he did not collect the ransom money was contradicted by Dr. Condon, the man who paid it over. His claim that he had nothing to do with the ladder used in the kidnapping was contradicted by Arthur Koehler, an expert from the United States Forest Products Laboratory, who identified part of its wood as coming from a board in Hauptmann's attic and part of it as a type stocked at a lumber yard in the Bronx, where Hauptmann had worked during the winter of 1931-1932 and where he had purchased $9.31 worth of lumber on December 29, 1931. Koehler further testified and demonstrated to the jury that markings on the kidnapping ladder were identical (even to imperfections) with markings made by a saw, plane, and chisel found in Hauptmann's possession. Hauptmann's claim that his prosperity at the time of the arrest was due to stock market operations was contradicted by the records of his brokerage accounts, showing losses. His claim of successful fur-trading operations with Fisch was contradicted by the testimony of Fisch's landlady and of his sister, showing that in the last years of his life, Fisch was a poor man, living in a cheap rented room and receiving financial help from his relatives in Germany.

As for defense attempts to corroborate Hauptmann's testimony, they boomeranged, sometimes disastrously. For example, his wife was asked about the cardboard box containing a large amount of ransom money which Hauptmann was supposed to have received from Fisch and left in the closet in his home. She said that she had never seen it. According to Hauptmann, who had testified just before her, it had been there from December 1933 to September 1934. The closet contained Mrs. Hauptmann's cleaning supplies and apron. She used it almost every day and cleaned it almost every week. Yet she never saw the cardboard box.

In contrast to the lack of corroboration for Hauptmann's story, the diverse threads of evidence that made up the prosecution's case fitted together into a pattern that was believable. Each thread was woven into every other, until the entire fabric had greater strength than any particular thread. Thus, Colonel Lindbergh's identification of Hauptmann's voice as the one that cried out, "Hey Doctor!" in St. Raymond's Cemetery, standing alone, was weak. But in the context of Dr. Condon's testimony that Hauptmann was the man that he met there that night, it gained strength.

This is not to suggest that the jurors were able to resolve contradictions between Hauptmann's testimony and that of the prosecution witnesses by the simple expedient of counting noses. Much more was involved: the interest of the witnesses, their individual characters, the inherent probability of their stories. But the jurors were able to rely on their own general experience for the knowledge that two or more persons telling the same story are more likely to be correct than one who is telling a contradictory story. Especially is this so if the many witnesses are not merely parroting each other, but telling what they know as the result of observations from several different vantage points.

Demeanor

In addition to the factors already discussed, and probably equally important in its influence on the jurors, was the matter of demeanor. What a witness says sometimes seems less significant than how he says it. His facial expression, the tone of his voice, the look in his eyes, the set of his jaw, his gestures —all these are clues as to whether he is worthy of belief. They may be grossly, even tragically, misinterpreted (for murderers sometimes look like angels and leading citizens like thugs), but their psychological impact is not to be denied. It is impossible here to do more than call attention to the importance of such factors, to note that they are more felt than reasoned about; and that they, too, must have contributed, rightly or wrongly, to the ultimate conclusion reached by the jurors in the Hauptmann case.

Balancing and Weighing the Evidence

The conclusion of the jury was that Hauptmann was lying. Exactly when it was reached is impossible to say. It is also impossible to be sure if the reasoning that led up to it bore any close resemblance to this imaginary and introspective attempt to re-create it. However, the jurors had the benefit of having the lawyers on both sides try to persuade them by discussing just such matters as those we have been considering, and they deliberated among themselves for eleven hours. These were occasions for expressing and examining the ideas that underlay their reasoning. If the ideas, when dragged out into the open and discussed, were found wanting, they could be discarded; if found good, they would bolster and confirm conclusions already tentatively reached.

Whatever the exact course of reasoning may have been, one thing seems clear: The verdict must have been reached on the basis of prior knowledge and experience—intellectual equipment that the jurors brought with them to the trial and that they possessed before it started. That was the sieve through which the evidence was screened, separating nuggets from dross.

Chapter / *Ten*

Circumstantial Evidence

Many decisions involve more than an appraisal of whether witnesses are telling the truth. They require that a conclusion be reached about events that even the witnesses have never observed. Such decisions are said to be based upon circumstantial evidence, meaning that inferences have to be drawn from known circumstances to hitherto unknown events.

What is the process of inference, and how does it work?

A brief answer would be that it is the type of mental operation used in the writing and reading of mystery stories, or the type that the jurors in the Hauptmann case must have used in appraising the prosecution's evidence—a matter only suggested in the preceding chapter.

The Trial of a Professor for Murder

Rather than discuss the Hauptmann case further, it may be more interesting to seek the answer in another famous trial, the prosecution in 1850 of Professor John W. Webster for the murder of Doctor George Parkman. Webster was a professor of chemistry at Harvard University and a lecturer at the Massachusetts Medical College. Parkman was a wealthy doctor who had founded the medical college and was active in its affairs.

Nobody who testified at the trial saw Parkman die. There were witnesses, however, who recounted the following circumstances:

Webster was having trouble living on his income. He had borrowed $400 from Parkman, and when unable to repay it, had borrowed $2000 more from Parkman and others, pledging as security his household furniture and a mineral collection he owned. Subsequently, he borrowed another $1200 from Parkman's brother-in-law on the security of the same mineral collection. Parkman, incensed at what he regarded as double-dealing, demanded payment and made no secret of his feelings. Webster promised to turn over the fees he received for lecturing at the medical college. When they were not paid Parkman pressed harder.

On Friday morning, November 23, 1849, Webster went to Parkman's home and made an appointment for Parkman to call that afternoon at the college. Parkman kept the appointment. That was the day he disappeared.

A widespread search ensued, during the course of which the neighborhood of the college was searched, including Webster's laboratory. The police officers were apologetic and diffident; they found nothing at the time.

Two days later, Webster called on Parkman's brother. After expressing rather perfunctory sympathy and concern, he made a special point of saying that Parkman had visited him at 1:30 P.M. on November 23, and received payment of $483 and some cents. Webster's meager bank account, however, showed no withdrawal.

Webster had sufficient interest in Parkman's disappearance to interview people who claimed to have seen Parkman on Friday afternoon after 2:00 P.M., but otherwise put in long hours in his laboratory behind closed and locked doors.

He would not even let the janitor in to build warming fires as was customary. Nevertheless, fires were burning in the laboratory day after day.

As a result of suspicions of the janitor, another search was made of Webster's laboratory and of the vault below it. This time the police discovered portions of a male body, including the charred remains of a set of false teeth. They also discovered blood-spattered trousers and slippers belonging to Webster.

The body had been skillfully dissected. It had not come from the dissecting rooms that adjoined Webster's laboratory, for there was no embalming fluid in the veins. From the structure of the limbs found, doctors were of the opinion that the body had been thin and tall, resembling that of Parkman. The false teeth were identified as Parkman's by the dentist who had made them.

When Webster was arrested and told that Parkman's body had been found he asked whether "the whole of the body" had been found. Later, brought to the college and confronted with the remains, he first disputed that the body was Parkman's and then attempted to throw suspicion on the janitor. Otherwise, he pleaded ignorance. Such was the evidence of the prosecution—all circumstantial.

Most of the defense evidence was of like nature. Twenty character witnesses, including the president of Harvard University and Oliver Wendell Holmes, Sr., testified that they had known Webster as a peaceable, gentle, and amiable man. Members of Webster's family testified that his behavior after Parkman's disappearance was perfectly normal: He spent his leisure in reading, gardening, and playing whist. Finally, a number of witnesses testified that they had seen Parkman at various places around Boston after 2 P.M. on the date of his disappearance.

Webster did not formally testify because of rules of evidence in effect at the time of his trial. He made a full oral statement (though not under oath and not subject to cross-examination), however, in which he protested his innocence and ignorance of the crime, and complained that his words and actions were being twisted. His statement (like Hauptmann's testimony and like the testimony of many defendants in criminal cases) was the only noncircumstantial information submitted to the jury.

The jurors found Webster guilty. How did they know what had happened between Webster and Parkman? By what authority did they disregard the statement of the one person living who was in a position to know definitely?

These questions seem rhetorical in light of the evidence. But the fact that they do provides a first generalization about circumstantial reasoning: it is largely subconscious. Convictions grow and decisions are reached without effort and without awareness of what is going on in one's mind. To that extent, the process closely resembles that of reasoning about credibility, discussed in the preceding chapter.

There is another obvious connection in that the circumstances from which inferences are made are themselves established by direct evidence. Thus the statements of the police officers as to what they found in Webster's laboratory and as to what he said must be believed before inferences can be drawn from these statements.

But after the circumstances have been established, how does the mind proceed? Even here the similarity is striking between circumstantial reasoning and reasoning about credibility. A certain fact is accepted by the decision-maker. To it he applies his pre-existing knowledge, and arrives at a tentative conclusion. Other tentative hypotheses spring from other facts. Gradually they coalesce, becoming less and less tentative. At some point a state of conviction is reached that satisfies the decision-maker to the extent that he is willing to act upon it. The only difference between such reasoning and that described in the preceding chapter is in the greater scope and variety of ideas used. They are not limited to credibility but extend potentially over the entire range of human knowledge.

One circumstance of importance in the Webster case was the simple fact that he was on trial. Had one of the jurors been questioned about its significance, he might have answered that there was none—that the defendant was presumed innocent until proven guilty. But pressed further, he might have agreed that the purpose of the presumption was only to enjoin caution upon him and his fellow jurors in listening to the evidence, and that its very existence was an indication that it was needed in order to counteract rational and natural inferences to the contrary. For the juror could hardly have denied that Webster's presence demonstrated the belief of prosecuting officials that Webster was guilty; otherwise, the man would not have been brought to trial. Nor could the juror have denied that the persons who had brought about that result comprised a substantial group of responsible citizens—members of the grand jury, lawyers in the district attorney's office, and police officials—or that the opinions of such people, based upon investigations and hearings, were more probably correct than incorrect. As a rational being, the juror would have difficulty in disregarding these facts, however anxious he might be to follow the judge's instructions and give effect to the presumption of innocence. A juror might or might not succeed in that endeavor. The inference would be tentative at most, not conclusive. The fact that Webster was on trial would not prove that he was guilty, but only that the probability of his guilt was greater than if he had not been on trial. Police officers, prosecutors, and members of the grand jury might all have been mistaken.

The ideas just outlined concern criminal cases in general and how they are brought to trial—the functions of police officers, prosecuting attorneys, and grand jurors, and the qualities of mind and heart of the people who perform such functions. Such ideas are not developed or even expressed during the trial, but are brought to it by the jurors as part of their ordinary mental equipment, gleaned from what they have learned and remembered from civics classes, newspaper reading, gossip, novels, in short, from their total life experiences.

When we return to formal evidence and inferences

that are legally permissible as well as rationally possible, one important piece of information was the fact that Webster was being hard pressed for the payment of his debt to Parkman. What was its relevancy? What significance did it have in showing whether Webster was guilty of murder?

It is unlikely that these questions were considered explicitly by the jurors. Probably their minds simply jumped to the conclusion that Webster had a motive for killing Parkman, and did so in a subconscious, lightning-like, inarticulated operation that took less time to perform than this sentence takes to read. The conclusion must have been based upon the store of ideas and beliefs pre-existing in the minds of the jurors with reference to the kind of fact that had been presented to them. As normal men, their minds were filled with thousands of bits of information and misinformation about the universe and things and people in it, including ideas about how people in debt feel and act. At this stage, it would have been extraordinary for the jurors to pause long enough to articulate the ideas they were using. The process involved no more conscious effort than breathing.

However, had the jurors been challenged on their inferential leap and asked to explain it, they might have said something like this: "If a man is hounded for a debt long enough and hard enough, he may become furious—so furious that he would like to kill his creditor."

Such an explanation would not be based on anything that happened at the trial. Nor would it be based upon research into the relationships between debtors and creditors or the motivations for crime. In all probability, it would be nothing more than a distillation of recollections by the jurors of their own hard times or speculative imaginings of the feelings of people about whom the jurors had read or heard. The generalization would express probability, not certainty, and it would be recognized as such. Possibly most debtors are grateful to their creditors and have no feeling other than apologetic remorse when they are unable to pay. Possibly murder or even the contemplation of it is rare in such situations. Nevertheless, there is sufficient ambiguity in the relations between debtors and creditors and there are enough murders for mercenary reasons to justify the generalization for *some* situations, and to say on that basis that there is *some probability* that Webster had a motive for killing Parkman. One cannot say that the chances are nine out of ten that Webster felt that way or even five out of ten, but only that there was some probability, enough to make the proposition more probable that Webster had the necessary motive than a proposition that a Mr. X—about whom nothing is known —had such a motive. That is enough to justify a very tentative conclusion.

It is possible logically to go on and infer from the motive the fact of the crime itself. But psychologically that is too big a step to take, and one's natural tendency is to await further evidence.

Each line of evidence follows substantially the same course as the one just traced. Starting with a fact supplied by a witness, the mind of the juror makes an inferential leap as far as his accumulated knowledge and experience about that type of fact permit. For example, the juror's mind would probably leap from the evidence of Webster's professional experience to the proposition that he had the capacity to commit the crime charged, and from the timing of Parkman's visit to the proposition that Webster had the opportunity to commit it. Other lines of inference may stem from direct perception by the jurors, as when Webster's blood-stained trousers and slippers were exhibited at the trial. Still other lines may start from the absence of evidence, for if there is no evidence of a certain possible state of affairs, it is fair to assume that it does not exist. Since there is no evidence suggesting the death of Parkman from natural causes, accident, or suicide, the inference is that his death resulted from foul play. This inference, like all others, expresses probabilities rather than certainties, and is based upon the pre-existing mass of ideas in the minds of the jurors—in this instance, those related to the possible causes of death and to the conduct of attorneys in litigation (their ability to find and produce relevant evidence).

All the various lines of proof and reasoning converge toward the ultimate fact in issue. In approaching it, the jurors may consciously put the lines together to see how they fit and whether jointly they support the conclusion tentatively reached before. The problem is to determine how probable it is that such a concurrence of facts as that presented to them could have happened fortuitously. If such a probability is slight, then it follows that the probability of their conclusion being true is high. Thus in Webster's case, the reasoning might have been as follows: If Parkman died by foul play (absence of evidence of suicide, accident, or natural causes) and Webster had a motive for killing him (a desire to get rid of a creditor who was harassing him) and also the opportunity (Parkman's visit) and the capacity to dispose of the body in the way it was done (neat dissection and burning); if Webster's conduct disclosed feelings of guilt (his lies about paying money to Parkman on the day of his disappearance; his mysterious operations behind closed doors; his curious question to the police as to whether the whole of Parkman's body had been found); and if no other explanation than Webster's guilt is apparent (again the absence of evidence), then it is highly probable that Webster committed the murder. In reaching or testing this final conclusion, jurors could not have been satisfied with a slight degree of probability, as in some of the intermediate steps of reasoning. They must have insisted upon a high degree, one which would satisfy the legal standard of being beyond a reasonable doubt.

That the jurors were not wrong was made clear by a rather exceptional incident after the trial. Webster, in one of his appeals for clemency while awaiting the death penalty, made the following statement:

On Tuesday, the 20th of November, I sent the note to Dr. Parkman, which, it appears, was carried by the boy Maxwell. I handed it to Littlefield unsealed. It was to ask Dr. Parkman to call at my rooms on Friday the 23d, after my lecture. He had become of late very importunate for his pay. He had threatened me with a suit, to put an officer into my house, and to drive me from my professorship, if I did not pay him. The purport of my note was simply to ask the conference. I did not tell him in it what I could do, or what I had to say about the payment. I wished to gain, for those few days, a release from his solicitations, to which I was liable every day on occasions and in a manner very disagreeable and alarming to me, and also to avert, for so long a time at least, the fulfilment of recent threats of severe measures. I did not expect to be able to pay him when Friday should arrive. My purpose was, if he should accede to the proposed interview, to state to him my embarrassments and utter inability to pay him at present, to apologize for those things in my conduct which had offended him, to throw myself upon his mercy, to beg for further time and indulgence for the sake of my family, if not for my own, and to make as good promises to him as I could have any hope of keeping.

I did not hear from him on that day, nor the next (Wednesday); but I found that on Thursday he had been abroad in pursuit of me, though without finding me. I feared that he had forgotten the appointment, or else did not mean to wait for it. I feared he would come in upon me at my lecture hours, or while I was preparing my experiments for it. Therefore, I called at his house on that morning (Friday), between eight and nine, to remind him of my wish to see him at the College at half-past one,—my lecture closing at one. I did not stop to talk with him then; for I expected the conversation would be a long one, and I had my lecture to prepare for. It was necessary for me to save my time, and also to keep my mind free from other exciting matters. Dr. Parkman agreed to call on me, as I proposed.

He came, accordingly, between half-past one and two. He came in at the lecture-room door. I was engaged in removing some glasses from my lecture-room table into the room in the rear, called the upper laboratory. He immediately addressed me with great energy: "Are you ready for me, sir? Have you got the money?" I replied, "No, Dr. Parkman;" and was then beginning to state my condition, and make my appeal to him.

He would not listen to me, but interrupted me with much vehemence. He called me "scoundrel" and "liar," and went on heaping upon me the most bitter taunts and opprobrious epithets. While he was talking, he drew a handful of papers from his pocket, and took from among them my two notes, and also an old letter from Dr. Hosack, written many years ago, and congratulating him (Dr. P.) on his success in getting me appointed professor of chemistry. "You see," he said, "I got you into your office, and now I will get you out of it." He put back into his pocket all the papers, except the letter and the notes. I cannot tell how long the torrent of threats and invectives continued, and I can now recall to memory but a small portion of what he said. At first I kept interposing, trying to pacify him, so that I might obtain the object for which I had sought the interview. But I could not stop him, and soon my own temper was up. I forgot everything. I felt nothing but the sting of his words. I was excited to the highest degree of passion; and while he was speaking and gesticulating in the most violent and menacing manner, thrusting the letter and his fist into my face, in my fury I seized whatever thing was handiest, —it was a stick of wood,—and dealt him an instantaneous blow with all the force that passion could give it. I did not know, nor think, nor care where I should hit him, nor how hard, nor what the effect would be. It was on the side of his head, and there was nothing to break the force of the blow. He fell instantly upon the pavement. There was no second blow. He did not move. I stooped down over him, and he seemed to be lifeless. Blood flowed from his mouth, and I got a sponge and wiped it away. I got some ammonia and applied it to his nose; but without effect. Perhaps I spent ten minutes in attempts to resuscitate him; but I found that he was absolutely dead. In my horror and consternation I ran instinctively to the doors and bolted them,—the doors of the lecture-room, and the laboratory below. And then, what was I to do?

It never occurred to me to go out and declare what had been done, and obtain assistance. I saw nothing but the alternative of a successful removal and concealment of the body, on the one hand, and of infamy and destruction on the other. The first thing I did, as soon as I could do anything, was to drag the body into the private room adjoining. There I took off the clothes, and began putting them into the fire which was burning in the upper laboratory. They were all consumed there that afternoon,—with papers, pocket-book, or whatever else they may have contained. I did not examine the pockets, nor remove anything except the watch. I saw that, or the chain of it, hanging out; and I took it and threw it over the bridge as I went to Cambridge.

My next move was to get the body into the sink which stands in the small private room. By setting the body partially erect against the corner, and getting up into the sink myself, I succeeded in drawing it up. There it was entirely dismembered. It was quickly done, as a work of terrible and desperate necessity. The only instrument used was the knife found by the officers in the tea-chest, and which I kept for cutting corks. . . .

While dismembering the body, a stream of Cochituate was running through the sink, carrying off the blood in a pipe that passed down through the lower laboratory. There must have been a leak in the pipe, for the ceiling below was stained immediately round it.

There was a fire burning in the furnace of the lower laboratory. Littlefield was mistaken in thinking there had never been a fire there. He had probably never kindled one, but I had done it myself several times. I had done it that day for the purpose of making oxygen gas. The head and viscera were put into that furnace that day, and the fuel heaped on. I did not examine at night to see to what degree they were consumed. Some of the extremities, I believe, were put in there on that day.

The pelvis and some of the limbs, perhaps all, were put under the lid of the lecture-room table in what is called the *well*,—a deep sink lined with lead. A stream of Cochituate was turned into it, and kept running through it all Friday night. The thorax was put into a similar well in the lower laboratory, which I filled with water, and threw in a quantity of potash which I found there. This disposition of the remains was not changed till after the visit of the officers on Monday.

When the body had been thus all disposed of, I cleared away all traces of what had been done. I took up the stick with which the fatal blow had been struck. It proved to be the stump of a large grape vine, say two inches in diameter, and two feet long. It was one of two or more pieces which I had carried in from Cambridge long before, for the purpose of showing the effect of certain chemical fluids in coloring wood, by being absorbed into the pores. The grape vine, being a very porous wood, was well suited to this purpose. Another longer stick had been used as intended, and exhibited to the students. This one had not been used. I put it into the fire.

I took up the two notes, either from the table or the floor, —I think the table,—close by where Dr. P. had fallen, I seized an old metallic pen lying on the table, dashed it across the face and through the signatures, and put them in my pocket. I do not know why I did this rather than put them into the fire; for I had not considered for a moment what effect either mode of disposing of them would have on the mortgage, or my indebtedness to Dr. P. and the other persons interested; and I had not yet given a single thought to the question as to what account I should give of the objects or results of my interview with Dr. Parkman. . . .

I left the College to go home, as late as six o'clock. I collected myself as well as I could, that I might meet my family and others with composure. On Saturday I visited my rooms at the College, but made no change in the disposition of the remains, and laid no plans as to my future course.

On Saturday evening I read the notice in the Transcript respecting the disappearance. I was then deeply impressed with the necessity of immediately taking some ground as to the character of my interview with Dr. P.: for I appointed it, first, by an unsealed note on Tuesday, and on Friday had myself called at his house in open day and ratified the arrangement, and had there been seen and probably overheard by the man-servant; and I knew not by how many persons Dr. P. might have been seen entering my rooms, or how many persons he might have told by the way where he was going. The interview would in all probability be known; and I must be ready to explain it. The question exercised me much; but on Sunday my course was taken. I would go into Boston, and be the first to declare myself the person, as yet unknown, with whom Dr. P. had made the appointment. I would take the ground, that I had invited him to the College to pay him money, and that I *had* paid him accordingly, I fixed upon the sum by taking the small note and adding interest, which, it appears, I cast erroneously. . . .

I looked into my rooms on Sunday afternoon, but did nothing.

After the first visit of the officers, I took the pelvis and some of the limbs from the upper well, and threw them into the vault under the privy. I took the thorax from the well below, and packed it in the tea-chest, as found. My own impression has been, that this was not done till after the second visit of the officers, which was on Tuesday; but Kingsley's testimony shows that it must have been done sooner. The perforation of the thorax had been made by knife at the time of removing the viscera.

On Wednesday, I put on kindlings and made a fire in the furnace below, having first poked down the ashes. Some of the limbs—I cannot remember what ones or how many—were consumed at that time. This was the last I had to do with the remains.[11]

This statement was not before the jurors when they reached their decision. Nevertheless, by applying their reasoning powers and general knowledge to the fragmentary facts presented at the trial, they were able to arrive at a substantially accurate picture of what had happened.

More Doubtful Verdicts

Verdicts are not always as accurate as in the Webster case. Occasionally this may be because of corruption on the part of a judge or a juror, but more often it is because of inherent difficulties in the fact-finding process. A trial is an attempt to reconstruct events that have happened in the past. Too often the materials for reconstruction are unequal to the task. Consider an auto accident. It happens in a split second, probably at night. There may be no witnesses who survive the accident, or if there are, their attention may have been directed elsewhere at the time, or they may have been so affected by shock and excitement that they failed to notice the little that was open to their observation. Yet months later, perhaps years later, a jury must attempt to decide what actually happened after hearing what these witnesses remember of what they saw. It is unlikely that any two of them will tell the same story. The evidence is unsatisfactory; nobody can find out what really happened; and yet the dispute must be decided one way or the other.

A Case of Mistaken Identity

Spectacular proof that even eyewitnesses can be mistaken is furnished by the case of Adolf Beck, who was tried in England in 1896 for a series of embezzlements. His claimed plan of operation was as follows: Posing as a titled man of wealth, he would strike up an acquaintance with a woman and persuade her that she should come to live with him either as his housekeeper or as his mistress. In making arrangements, he would suggest that her clothes and jewelry were not adequate to her approaching new status and give her a check to purchase new clothes, and he would borrow a ring so that he would have the measurements for ordering better jewelry. Occasionally, he would also take along a bracelet to be repaired and sometimes he would borrow change for cabfare. The articles and money were never returned; the checks bounced; the man disappeared. No fewer than ten of the victims (eyewitnesses of course) positively identified Beck as the embezzler, and he was convicted. Upon his release from prison, another series of embezzlements following the same pattern occurred, and again Beck was arrested and convicted, this time in 1904. Then while Beck was in jail, the real embezzler was caught—an entirely different man, but one who looked and dressed very much like Beck. Beck was pardoned.

Other similar instances can be cited. A recent example is the case of Bertram Campbell who was tried in New York for passing forged checks. He was convicted on the basis of eyewitness testimony by bank tellers who identified him as the check passer. After years in prison (he was sentenced to a term of five to ten years), the real culprit was found and Campbell was released. The New York State legislature awarded him $155,000 as compensation for what he had suffered as a result of the mistake, but he died before having much chance to enjoy it.

The Value of Circumstantial Evidence

The contrast between such cases and the Webster case sharply challenges popular notions about the value of circumstantial evidence. Since Beck's case and Campbell's case were wrongly decided on the basis of direct evidence and Webster's case correctly decided on the basis of circumstantial evidence, the conclusion would seem to be that circumstantial evidence does not deserve the bad name it bears.

Such a conclusion may seem startling to laymen, but it is commonplace for judges and lawyers. They know from experience that without it criminal prosecutions would grind to a halt. Murder is rarely committed in the presence of witnesses and so must be proved, if it is to be proved at all, by inferences from circumstantial evidence—threats uttered to the victim by the accused, the accused's possession of the murder weapon, and the like. What is true of murder is also true of many other kinds of crime—disinterested eyewitnesses are simply not available and the only direct evidence to be had is that which comes from the lips of the accused. Even when disinterested eyewitnesses are available, they inevitably stop short of what is often the most crucial aspect of the crime to which they testify—the intention or motive with which it was committed. Such mental state, if it is to be proved at all, must be proved by circumstantial evidence, by the words and conduct of the accused, rather than by any direct look into his skull.

Jurors, happily, are usually unaware of their use of circumstantial evidence when they accept fingerprint, ballistic, or other types of such evidence. They consider that they are merely applying their commonsense. That, indeed, is exactly what they are doing—using their innate logic and their accumulated knowledge and experience to appraise the facts presented to them in court.

Some responsible and informed observers believe that circumstantial evidence is not only useful but better than direct evidence. Martin M. Frank, judge and former prosecuting attorney, expressed this view as follows:

> Circumstantial evidence is not a vague, amorphous thing, as popularly conceived, which, chameleon-like, can change in varying connotations to suit the occasion. It is, in truth, an essential component of legal procedure, and I assert unequivocally and emphatically that when it is available in adequate measure there is no more convincing or trustworthy proof.
>
> Nor do I stand alone in this view. The highest courts in every jurisdiction in our country, and in Great Britain as well, have so held.[12]

Charlie Chaplin's Paternity Case

Sometimes the circumstantial evidence is clear and conclusive, but its significance misunderstood by judge or jury or both. Perhaps that is what hapened in a paternity suit brought against Charlie Chaplin in California during the Second World War. Miss Joan Berry sued to have him declared the father of her infant child and to force him to pay support money. She testified to several acts of sexual intercourse with Chaplin at about the time the child must have been conceived. Chaplin admitted intercourse several months earlier, but denied it at or near the crucial date. His principal defense, however, was that the blood tests of himself, Miss Berry, and the child showed conclusively that he could not have been the father. The blood tests were made by three reputable physicians whose competency and integrity were never questioned. They reported in writing that:

> Examination of the bloods of Charles Chaplin, Joan Berry and Carol Ann Berry give the following results.

	GROUP	TYPE
Charles Chaplin	O	MN
Joan Berry	A	N
Carol Ann Berry	B	N

> Conclusion reached as the result of these blood grouping tests is that in accordance with the well-accepted laws of heredity, the man, Charles Chaplin, cannot be the father of the child, Carol Ann Berry. The law of heredity which applies here is "The agglutinogens A and B cannot appear in the blood of a child unless present in the blood of one or both parents."

Medical testimony at the trial reiterated the findings of the report that Charles Chaplin could not have been the father of the child. No contrary scientific evidence was offered in rebuttal. Yet the jury brought in a verdict against the defendant, which was sustained on appeal.[18] It would seem that the jurors could not have understood the doctors, for there was no rational ground for disbelieving their testimony.

But perhaps there is another explanation: prejudice. Charlie Chaplin was reputed to be not only extremely wealthy and a libertine but also a slacker in America's war effort. He remained a British subject despite long residence in the United States, and he did not join with other movie stars in USO shows and similar entertainments provided for troops. These were serious charges during the Second World War, and because the trial was a notorious one, they were the subject of extensive journalistic comment and prejudging as well as common gossip. These influences may well have surrounded and pervaded the atmosphere of the courtroom and poisoned the minds of the jurors. Such an explanation is not implausible, for American courts, unlike those in England, have not yet found any satisfactory formula for controlling mob psychology and mass hysteria directed toward pending cases. Certainly there have been cases both before the Charlie Chaplin trial and after it where results have been suspect because of the atmosphere in which trials were conducted. Classic examples, to mention only two, are the Sacco-Vanzetti case ("Bolsheviks" convicted of murder) and the Scottsboro case (several young Negroes convicted of raping two white women in the Deep South). One of the interesting things about such cases is that it is seldom logic that is at fault, but usually the premises upon which logic operates. If one starts with the proposition that Negroes and Bolsheviks should be put out of the way regardless of whether they have committed any crimes, the conclusions reached in those cases are inescapable. But if one starts with the proposition that no Negro or Bolshevik should be convicted and punished for crime, then contrary conclusions are equally inescapable. The logic in both instances is unassailable, but the major premises are both defective. So again we see pre-existing ideas controlling decisions. Logic takes care of itself as a natural functioning of the normal mind. Aristotle himself could have done no better than the jurors in the Sacco-Vanzetti and Scottsboro cases if he had started with their ideas.

Perhaps there is still another possible explanation for the Charlie Chaplin decision. It may be that the jurors understood the medical evidence perfectly and believed it; that they had no animus toward Charlie Chaplin but instead nostalgic affection for him because of the laughs he had given them in the past; and that they would have rendered a like decision against any man in the same circumstances. Perhaps their reasoning was that a man ought to be held responsible for the support of any child he might have sired even if he is not, in fact, the biological father. He takes certain risks along with his pleasures, including the risk that the lady in question may honor him, rather than some other recipient of her favors, with responsibility. That such may have been in fact the reasoning of the jury is suggested by the action of other juries in other paternity cases. A qualified and experienced observer of such cases has remarked that:

> It is easier to convict a man of paternity in the United States than it is to convict him of a five-dollar traffic violation. The accusing woman has only to point a finger; not one of our states requires any supporting evidence or corroboration of her charge. Unless a blood test clears him—a possibility that varies with blood type but gives an innocent man a 50-50 chance on the average—the woman's word alone makes the case. As a result, 30 to 40 percent of the men convicted are innocent; and aware of the odds against them, thousands more submit to blackmail rather than face court proceedings. . . .
>
> Our laws reflect our basic social attitudes. The unwed mother, publicly revealing her shame in order to secure support for her helpless baby, is naturally an object of deep sympathy. The presumption has traditionally been strong against the man she names. Also, many of our courts seem to be guided by the maxim, "If the real father can't be found, anyone will do." [14]

The effect of the Charlie Chaplin decision, whatever its intention, was to hold a man who had been intimate with a woman responsible for the support of her child by some other man. If that was also the intention (and how else can the decision of the appellate court, approving the verdict, be explained?), then we are confronted not with mistake, ignorance, or prejudice, but with the evolution of a new rule of law—a matter to be discussed in the succeeding two chapters. The fact that the change in law is unacknowledged does not alter its character.

Chapter / Eleven

Fitting the Law
to the Facts

Thus far we have talked about decisions of questions of fact as if they were made in a vacuum. Such is not the case, of course. They are practical, made for the purpose of determining what legal consequences, if any, should follow—whether in a criminal case the defendant should be punished, or whether in a civil case he should be made to pay damages or some equivalent. This purpose sometimes colors and distorts the fact-finding process, as we shall see in the next chapter. First, however, it is important to try to understand what is involved in deciding an issue of law.

The process is not fundamentally different from that of deciding an issue of fact. Again, pre-existing ideas are applied to accepted facts to reach a conclusion. The main differences lie in the increased consciousness of the process and the type of pre-existing ideas used.

In the Hauptmann case the jurors probably had little difficulty with law. The question was whether the conduct of the defendant should be characterized as murder, and the answer was provided in general terms by the judge's instructions. Even without instructions, however, the jurors could have managed. The idea of murder is so common that it is part of the mental equipment of laymen as well as lawyers. As Judge Curtis Bok has remarked: "Murder, robbery, assault, rape, and fraud have been quite well understood since the days of Julius Caesar."

In the Webster case, the problem was more difficult, for the jurors had to choose between murder and manslaughter. The guidance they received from the judge was in these words:

> In seeking for the sources of our law upon this subject, it is proper to say, that whilst the statute law of the Commonwealth declares (Rev. Stat. c. 125, Section 1), "that every person who commits the crime of murder shall suffer the punishment of death for the same," yet it nowhere defines the crimes of murder or manslaughter, with all their minute and carefully-considered distinctions and qualifications. For these, we resort to that great repository of rules, principles, and forms, the common law. . . .
>
> Murder, in the sense in which it is now understood, is the killing of any person in the peace of the Commonwealth, with *malice aforethought,* either express or implied by law. Malice, in this definition, is used in a technical sense, including not only anger, hatred, and revenge, but every other unlawful and unjustifiable motive. It is not confined to ill-will towards one or more individual persons, but is intended to denote an action, flowing from any wicked and corrupt motive, any thing done *malo animo,* where the fact has been attended with such circumstances as carry in them the plain indications of a heart regardless of social duty, and fatally bent upon mischief. And therefore malice is implied from any deliberate or cruel act against another, however sudden.
>
> Manslaughter is the unlawful killing of another without malice; and may be either voluntary, as when the act is committed with a real design and purpose to kill, but through the violence of sudden passion, occasioned by some great provocation, which in tenderness for the frailty of human nature the law considers sufficient to palliate the criminality of the offence; or involuntary, as when the death of another is caused by some unlawful act, not accompanied by any intention to take life.[15]

This language is less enlightening than it might be. If it was not understood by the jurors there was no irreparable loss, for they could fall back upon their own ideas, fuzzy though they might be, as to the distinction between murder and manslaughter. At least, the jurors must have grasped the main point: murder was the more serious of the two offenses. Knowing that a verdict of murder would lead to the death penalty whereas a verdict of manslaughter would lead only to imprisonment, they probably had their own ideas as to which punishment was more appropriate for Webster. When a judge's instructions fail in their purpose of communicating ideas to the jury, they tend to become mere ritual. Instead of keeping the jurors within the boundaries of legal rules, their effect is to remove all restraints and to encourage the jurors to follow their own conceptions of justice.

Whether the general ideas of murder and manslaughter used in the Webster case were derived from the judge's instruction or dredged out of the jurors' own minds, the application of them to the mental picture the jurors formed of Webster's conduct was not dissimilar to the job they had in deciding upon the credibility of witnesses, or in putting circumstances together and drawing inferences from them. These operations also involved the application of general preexisting ideas to accepted facts.

There were two differences, however. The first has already been mentioned: The jurors did not necessarily have to reach down into their own personal store of knowledge and experience for the general ideas to be used. The judge's instructions were meant to supply them. Second, the ideas themselves were different from those used in factual reasoning. They were ethical concepts, distinguishing between good and evil, characterizing conduct as blameworthy or praiseworthy, and looking toward what ought to be done in view of the situation found to exist.

Law consists of a large, complex collection of such ideas, covering hundreds of thousands of situations (though by no means all that can and do arise). Each rule states the factual conditions for granting or withholding legal action. Just as the rule on murder states the factual conditions for imposing punishment, so the law of contracts provides that if a man makes a promise (condition one) that is supported by consideration (condition two) and fails to fulfill it (condition three), thereby causing loss to the other party (condition four), then (here comes the legal action) he shall become liable to pay damages. This is a gross oversimplification, of course, but sufficient to reveal the nature of rules of law. Such rules are expressed in constitutions, statutes, ordinances, regulations, judicial opinions, and scholarly writings; and they are systematically preserved and catalogued. In this respect also, they present a striking contrast to the uncatalogued, unsystematized, unrecorded, and unindexed jumble of hunches and premises that underlie everyday factual reasoning.

A Euthanasia Case

The problem of deciding a question of law is not always as simple as it was in the Webster case. If, for example, the Webster jurors had been confronted with a mercy killing instead of one prompted by bad temper and mercenary motives, they might have experienced much more difficulty. Such a case arose in New Hampshire in 1950 when Dr. R. H. Sander was charged with having deliberately and fatally injected air into the veins of a dying patient who was suffering from incurable cancer. At his trial for murder the defense was that the doctor's mind had "snapped" and, besides, that the patient was already dead when the injection was made. A medical record made by the doctor eight days later, supporting the charge against him, was explained as a mistake. The doctor was acquitted. (About a month later, however, the state medical board suspended his license to practice medicine on the ground that his conduct was "morally reprehensible.")

Auto Accident Cases

Similar examples are readily at hand in auto accident cases, which occupy so much of the time of the courts today. Typical of the situations presented in such cases is one where the driver beats a traffic light about to turn red and runs down a pedestrian who has stepped off the curb just a moment too soon. For purposes of analysis, let us assume such a case, and that the judge instructs the jury to find for the plaintiff if the defendant's negligence was the *sole* cause of the plaintiff's injuries. He defines negligence as the failure to exercise that degree of care which a reasonable man would exercise under the same circumstances.

Despite its apparent simplicity, the case is not an easy one. While the law is settled and not unduly complicated in its verbal formulation, it is neither specific nor universally acceptable. Not everyone would agree that fault should be the controlling factor in deciding whether a person injured in an auto accident should receive compensation, or that he should be barred from recovery because of comparatively slight negligence on his part.

The jury's first job is to determine whether either party is guilty of negligence. Is a pedestrian negligent because he doesn't wait for a clear green light before starting to cross the street? Is an automobile driver negligent because he doesn't come to a stop when the light is changing? The judge's instructions do not provide specific answers, but merely say that the conduct of the parties should be judged by the standard of what an imaginary reasonable man would do in the same circumstances.

This is not much help. As A. P. Herbert said:

There has never been a problem, however difficult, which His Majesty's judges have not in the end been able to resolve by asking themselves the simple question, "Was this or was it not the conduct of a reasonable man?" and leaving that question to be answered by the jury.[16]

Consequently, the jurors are forced to rely on their own ethical ideas. Fortunately, they have such ideas, derived from many diverse sources: gossip, school, personal driving and walking experiences, learning what judges and juries have done in other lawsuits. Some of the ideas are clearly value judgments (like the idea that a man shouldn't rush a traffic light) while others seem more purely factual in nature (like the idea that a traffic light changes every few seconds). Those relevant to appraising the driver's conduct might be something as follows: (1) He could have come to a stop before reaching the traffic light; (2) Waiting until the light was green would not have delayed him for more than a few seconds; (3) He could have anticipated a pedestrian crossing the street; (4) He could have slowed his speed to a point where he could have stopped within a few feet; and (5) He could have sounded his horn. Applying such ideas to the facts, the jury probably would conclude that the driver was negligent. The intellectual process is almost identical to that involved in circumstantial reasoning and in reasoning about credibility. The only difference lies in the particular ideas used.

The same type of reasoning would be applicable to the pedestrian's conduct. Rather than spell it out, we may assume that the jury would believe that the risk of danger in stepping out from a curb without first making sure that no cars were coming was not justified by the few seconds that might be saved, and consequently that the pedestrian also was negligent.

The difficulty is that his conduct does not seem as bad as the driver's. The pedestrian was imperiling only his own life, not anyone else's. Nevertheless, the judge said that any negligence on the part of the plaintiff, even though less than the negligence of the defendant, should bar recovery. That is the legal rule.

Do the jurors have to apply it and render a verdict for the driver? Should they, even if they are in no danger of being thrown into jail if they don't? That depends upon what they conceive their job to be. Is it to do justice or to apply rules that they believe to be unjust? They have their own ideas on that subject, too, which the judge probably didn't try to change.

Whatever jurors ought to do, apparently most of them don't apply the rule of contributory negligence, if reputable and experienced judges are to be believed. Here are the observations of one such man, Judge Joseph N. Ulman of the trial bench of Baltimore:

Somebody has been hurt in an accident. He sues another, charging that the accident was caused by that other's negligence. He proves conclusively that the defendant was negligent. But, if the evidence shows that the plaintiff was negligent, too, and that the accident would not have happened except for the negligence of both plaintiff and defendant, then, according to the law-in-the-law-books, the verdict of the jury must be for the defendant. The judge gives the jury that instruction, and adds that it does not make any difference whose negligence was the greater. If the plaintiff was careless to ever so slight a degree, and if the defendant was absolutely reckless, still the verdict must be for the defendant.

That is the law-in-the-law-books. It has been the law ever since 1809 when an English judge said so, in what has become a great leading case. Most American lawyers, I feel sure, think of this as not merely "the law," but as something essentially right and just and philosophically inevitable. That is the effect upon their thought processes of having eyes in the back of their heads. Do not blame the lawyers for the peculiar anatomical change that they have suffered. They have to wear their eyes that way if they are to be successful in finding the precedents and in telling you the law-in-the-law-books when you go to them for advice.

Sometimes, however, the effect is disastrous. For example, don't let any lawyer tell you that the law of contributory negligence is what I have just said it is. At least, don't let him tell you that this is the law of contributory negligence as it really works in the court room, and as it will affect your rights or your liabilities in a real case. Probably he will not even think of telling you so because even trained lawyers have observed that juries have knocked this theoretical law of contributory negligence into a cocked hat. For many years, juries have been deciding cases just as though there was no such rule of law. And all the time judges have been going on saying gravely that there is. Anyone with open eyes directed either to the front or to the rear, can plainly see that, on this point at least, the living law is jury-made far more truly than it is judge-made.

My note books leave me in no doubt about it. Still keeping to the field of traffic cases, I find one after another in which the suit is for damage to an automobile. The amount of such damage is perfectly definite. Nobody disputes the fact that it cost, say two hundred dollars, to repair the damaged automobile in each of three cases. In one case, the jury brings in a verdict for one hundred dollars. In the next, the verdict is for one hundred and fifty dollars. In the third, it is for twenty-five dollars. Does that mean that the three juries have been shaking dice or tossing coins to reach their verdicts? Not at all. Examine carefully the evidence in each case, and you will find that in the first the evidence showed that plaintiff and defendant were about equally careless. In the second, both were at fault, but the defendant was almost wholly responsible for the collision. In the third, the plaintiff was very careless, but the defendant was just a shade worse than the plaintiff.

Those are three supposed cases, but they are typical. More often the case is one in which very substantial damages have been proved, but damages not exactly measurable in money. The plaintiff has suffered for weeks or months as a result of an accident. The jury gives him a verdict that barely covers his bills from the doctor. Examine the evidence carefully and you find that both parties were careless. The jury has balanced the carelessness of one against the carelessness of the other and expressed the result in a small verdict.

What has the jury done, then, to the law of contributory negligence? It has simply remade it in a way that strikes jurors as being more sensible than the way it was made by a judge in 1809 and followed and elaborated by other judges during the one hundred and twenty-three years since that time. The strange part of it is that in the classical lawbooks you will not find a single word even hinting that the law of contributory negligence is what it has become by this habitual action of juries. This is because the men who write these lawbooks have not troubled themselves to look at the law as a living organism, as it actually works in the court room. They, like the other members of the legal profession, have riveted their eyes upon the past, and upon the printed page.[17]

Coming back to our hypothetical case, there may be additional factors in the case which seem important to the jurors. They may know that the defendant is insured (probably this was discovered when they were questioned as to their fitness to serve as jurors, or when a witness for the defendant was identified as a claims adjuster for an insurance company); or they may merely suspect that he is, because so many motorists are; or they may be of the view that he should be insured —otherwise he should not be permitted to drive. If so, especially in view of the fact that his fault seems to be greater than the plaintiff's, they may think it just to render a verdict against him. This is on the theory that if he carries insurance the loss will be spread among thousands of policyholders instead of concentrated with crushing force on the injured party; or if he is not insured, he should be made an example of, so that other uninsured motorists will take heed.

Such ideas may prevail even if the judge tells the jurors to disregard insurance completely. His comments and the legal rules that he lays down to that effect may seem to the jurors just as wrong as the rule on contributory negligence, and just as inconsistent with their duty as they conceive it, to do justice. So they may render a verdict in favor of the pedestrian.

Even if the jurors had to make explicit findings (as happens occasionally when a special verdict is used or interrogatories are submitted), they could accomplish the desired result by making findings consistent with the over-all conclusion to be reached. For example, they might say that the plaintiff was not negligent, or even that he did not step out into the street when he did. This suggests the interaction between factual conclusions and legal conclusions, to be developed more fully in the next chapter. All intermediate decisions—those relating to the credibility of witnesses, to the probative force of circumstantial evidence, and to intermediate legal or ethical judgments—are tentative and subject to reconsideration until a decision is announced. The over-all net result is likely to seem so important to the person making the decision that he will retrace his steps and reconsider any tentative conclusion that seems to lead away from where he conceives justice to lie. This is no great effort or strain upon intellectual integrity, because most reasoning, as pointed out before, is not conscious or explicit. In fact, the shock of approaching an end result that seems unjust may be the very challenge that causes a man to articulate and examine closely his underlying ideas.

The point of this excursion into what some lawyers and judges consider irrational jury behavior is to emphasize the crucial importance of pre-existing ideas in the process of decision-making. Not only are such ideas used to fill gaps in the law (as in the decision on negligence) but also sometimes to override positive rules of law (like the rule of contributory negligence and the one making insurance immaterial). Indeed it is probably no exaggeration to say that the only rules of law that juries apply consistently are those which do not offend their own pre-existing store of ethical ideas. That, in large part, is the explanation for the historic failure of prohibition —most juries simply wouldn't convict.

In criminal cases juries have the power to disregard rules of law completely by acquitting defendants who they believe should not be punished. When they acquit, judges are powerless to intervene. In civil cases, the freedom of juries is limited by the power of judges to direct verdicts whenever they believe that reasonable men could reach only one conclusion on the evidence and the law. But even in such cases, juries enjoy a wide latitude to determine for themselves the concrete meaning of rules of law. This is because many, if not most, rules, whether judge-made or found in statutes, are like the law of negligence already discussed—extremely general and vague. Such rules do not provide specific answers for particular fact situations but merely point in a general direction. What they mean as applied to an actual specific fact pattern is left for the jury to say. In some cases, there is no dispute as to what happened; all parties are agreed that such and such events took place. And yet the result is not clear, because the law itself does not supply an answer tailor-made to the specific facts involved. The result is that the answer is supplied by a jury.

Such reasoning as we have imagined in the auto accident case is not the result of mental aberration. It is perfectly logical, given the ideas that the jurors start with. Nor are the ideas themselves inherently absurd. Some legislatures have enacted them into law, for there are statutes in some places that abolish the rule of contributory negligence in favor of a doctrine of comparative negligence, in others that allow insurance companies to be sued directly, others that establish in place of traditional rules of fault a system of compensation for automobile accidents similar to that which generally prevails for industrial accidents. Once such ideas find their way into statute books they become respectable and no longer seem absurd.

Judges and lawyers have no monopoly on ethical ideas as to what should be done in situations coming before the courts. Insofar as they leave decision-making to jurors, they have little cause to be surprised to find that jurors sometimes use other ethical ideas than those embodied in legal rules.

How Judges Decide Questions of Law

Judges themselves reason in much the same fashion as jurors. They, too, do interstitial rule-making, just as a jury does when it defines negligence for a particular factual situation. They, too, sometimes disregard old rules which they find to be unjust. Happily, most of them do not lose their ethical ideas when they graduate from law school or ascend to the bench. They are men first and judges second. In fact, most judges who are generally considered great—men like Oliver Wendell Holmes, Jr., and Benjamin Nathan Cardozo—are ones who possessed lively and vigorous ethical ideas outside of the legal rules of their time. Because of such ideas they were able to plow new paths in the law.

Judges differ from juries chiefly in two respects. First, they possess a special body of ideas not shared by jurors about existing rules of law and their value and importance as precedents. They tend to think it wrong to disturb the existing structure of legal rules too radically or too quickly. This makes them more circumscribed and less flexible than jurors. Second, they articulate their ethical ideas and their relationships to existing rules in the form of judicial opinions, which in turn become precedents for subordinate and future judges. The necessity of doing this makes judges more conscious than jurors of the effect of their decisions upon future situations beyond the ones immediately before them.

But the landmarks of the law, the leading cases, are not ones in which judges have merely reiterated old rules. They are ones in which judges have filled gaps in existing law or overruled prior decisions. In these cases the judges necessarily have used ideas beyond those already embalmed in existing rules.

A question of law to be resolved by judicial decision usually arises in the pleading stage of a case. A plaintiff alleges certain facts and asks a remedy because of them. The court must decide whether he is entitled to it. Or the defendant alleges certain facts which he claims exonerate him from liability. The court must decide whether he is right. In either instance, the court assumes the facts *as stated* and determines what legal consequences follow from this.

Sometimes, however, the decision of a question of law is postponed until the trial stage. When that happens, issues of fact and law tend to become entangled, but the court is required to determine the legal consequences of facts, not as merely stated or assumed, but as established by the evidence. The initial decision of the trial judge may take the form of instructions to the jury, or a ruling upon a motion for a directed verdict. In either case, it will be subject to appellate review, just as a ruling on a pleading question would be. The appellate court decision is the one that will fix the law for the future.

Two Parallel Cases

That judges reason in substantially the same manner as jurors is neatly illustrated in two parallel cases which arose early in this century.

In 1909, E. Wells Johnson bought a Cadillac automobile from a dealer in Utica, New York. At about the same time, in the neighboring city of Schenectady, New York, Donald C. MacPherson bought a Buick automobile from a dealer. Both automobiles turned out to be defective. In each instance, a wheel collapsed while the car was being driven slowly, and the owner was injured.

Each owner sued the manufacturer of his automobile to recover damages. But the cases were tried in different courts —Johnson's case in a federal district court in New York and MacPherson's case in a state court in New York.

At the time of trial there was no clear-cut legal rule in either court on the precise situation presented. Plenty of analogies were available, cases where people had sued manufacturers from whom they had bought directly, cases where people had purchased merchandise other than automobiles from dealers and then sued the manufacturers, even cases in other jurisdictions involving automobiles where the ultimate

consumer had sued the manufacturer, but there was no binding precedent in either court on the precise problem to be
decided.

At the trial court level, both Johnson and MacPherson
won. That meant that in each case the judge and jury decided
that the ultimate consumer of a defective automobile should
recover from the negligent manufacturer, even though the car
was purchased from a dealer and not from the manufacturer
directly.

Both cases were appealed. Johnson's case reached the
United States Circuit Court of Appeals in March of 1915.
After reviewing analogous cases, that court reversed the judg-
ment below in an opinion which concluded that:

> One who manufactures articles inherently dangerous, e.g.,
> poisons, dynamite, gunpowder, torpedoes, bottles of water un-
> der gas pressure, is liable in tort to third parties which they
> injure, unless he prove that he has exercised reasonable care
> with reference to the article manufactured. [Citations]. . . .
> On the other hand, one who manufactures articles dangerous
> only if defectively made, or installed, e.g., tables, chairs, pic-
> tures or mirrors hung on the walls, carriages, automobiles, and
> so on, is not liable to third parties for injuries caused by them,
> except in case of willful injury or fraud. [Citations]

In so deciding, the court necessarily made new law to
cover the precise situation presented. The ethical ideas that
induced it to so rule are not spelled out in the opinion and
may never have been discussed even by the judges themselves
in private conferences on the case. One judge, however, dis-
sented, and he brought his ethical ideas out into the open. Said
he:

> The principles of law invoked by the defendant had their
> origin many years ago, when such a delicately organized
> machine as the modern automobile was unknown. Rules appli-
> cable to stage coaches and farm implements become archaic
> when applied to a machine which is capable of running with

safety at the rate of 50 miles an hour. I think the law as it exists today makes the manufacturer liable if he sells such a machine under a direct or implied warranty that he has made, or thoroughly inspected, every part of the machine, and it goes to pieces because of rotten material in one of its most vital parts, which the manufacturer never examined or tested in any way. If, however, the law be insufficient to provide a remedy for such negligence it is time that the law should be changed. "New occasions teach new duties"; situations never dreamed of 20 years ago are now of almost daily occurrence.

The law should be construed to cover the conditions produced by a new and dangerous industry, and should provide redress for such injuries as the plaintiff has sustained. My own judgment is, considering the dangers to be encountered from passenger automobiles, that the manufacturer is under an implied obligation to build such cars of materials capable of doing the work required of them. He may purchase the parts of makers of high reputation, but this does not absolve him from the obligation of a personal inspection, which at least will discover obvious defects, such as decayed and "dozy" spokes. If it be impossible for the manufacturer to inspect the wheels at his own place of business he should have a representative skilled in the business at the wheel factory to make such inspection. In other words, where the lives and limbs of human beings are at stake it is not enough for the manufacturer to assert that he bought the wheel, which collapsed four months after it was sold, from a reputable maker and thought it was made of sound material. Such an excuse might be sufficient in the case of a farm wagon or a horse drawn vehicle of any kind, but in my opinion, it is wholly insufficient in the case of a wagon propelled by gasoline, which is capable of making 50 miles an hour.[18]

For procedural reasons, not of present concern, Johnson's case was sent back to the trial court for further proceedings.

At about the same time, MacPherson's case reached the New York Court of Appeals. The opinion of that court is a famous one written by Benjamin N. Cardozo. Like the opinion in the Johnson case it reviews analogous cases, and like the Johnson opinion concludes (though without quite saying so directly) that there is no controlling precedent for the precise situation before the court. Then, however, it proceeds to reach a conclusion diametrically opposed to that reached by the federal court in the Johnson case. The gist of it is contained in these words:

> We hold, then, that the principle of *Thomas v. Winchester* is not limited to poisons, explosives, and things of like nature, to things which in their normal operation are implements of destruction. If the nature of a thing is such that it is reasonably certain to place life and limb in peril when negligently made, it is then a thing of danger. Its nature gives warning of the consequences to be expected. If to the element of danger there is added knowledge that the thing will be used by persons other than the purchaser, and used without new tests, then, irrespective of contract, the manufacturer of this thing of danger is under a duty to make it carefully.

The ethical ideas that induced this choice between two alternatives are suggested by Judge Cardozo in the following passages:

> Beyond all question, the nature of an automobile gives warning of probable danger if its construction is defective. This automobile was designed to go fifty miles an hour. Unless its wheels were sound and strong, injury was almost certain. It was as much a thing of danger as a defective engine for a railroad. The defendant knew the danger. It knew also that the car would be used by persons other than the buyer. This was apparent from its size; there were seats for three persons. It was apparent also from the fact that the buyer was a dealer in cars, who bought to resell. The maker of this car supplied it for the use of purchasers from the dealer just as plainly as the contractor in *Devlin v. Smith* supplied the scaffold for use by the servants of the owner. The dealer was indeed the one person of whom it might be said with some approach to certainty that by him the car would not be used. Yet the defendant would have us say that he was the one person whom it was under a

legal duty to protect. The law does not lead us to so inconsequent a conclusion. Precedents drawn from the days of travel by stage coach do not fit the conditions of travel today. The principle that the danger must be imminent does not change, but the things subject to the principle do change. They are whatever the needs of life in a developing civilization require them to be. . . .

We think the defendant was not absolved from a duty of inspection because it bought the wheels from a reputable manufacturer. It was not merely a dealer in automobiles, it was a manufacturer of automobiles. It was responsible for the finished product. It was not at liberty to put the finished product on the market without subjecting the component parts to ordinary and simple tests.

In this case also there was a dissent, this time by a judge who preferred the result reached in the Johnson case as more consistent with what he conceived to be the over-all trend of legal decisions in analogous cases. His remarks on the Johnson case are especially interesting:

That the Federal courts still adhere to the general rule, as I have stated it, appears by the decision of the Circuit Court of Appeals in the Second Circuit, in March, 1915, in the case of *Cadillac Motor Car Co. v. Johnson* (221 Fed. Rep. 801). That case, like this, was an action by a subvendee against a manufacturer of automobiles for negligence in failing to discover that one of its wheels was defective, the court holding that such an action could not be maintained. It is true there was a dissenting opinion in that case, but it was based chiefly upon the proposition that rules applicable to stage coaches are archaic when applied to automobiles and that if the law did not afford a remedy to strangers to the contract the law should be changed. If this be true, the change should be effected by the legislature and not by the courts. A perusal of the opinion in that case and in the *Huset* case will disclose how uniformly the courts throughout this country have adhered to the rule and how consistently they have refused to broaden the scope of the exceptions. I think we should adhere to it in the case at bar and, therefore, I vote for a reversal of this judgment.[19]

The story is not finished yet. By a peculiar quirk of fate, the Johnson case came back again to the United States Circuit Court of Appeals. The lower court had obediently followed the rule laid down in the earlier decision and dismissed the complaint. This time the plaintiff appealed. When the United States Circuit Court of Appeals came to consider the case for the second time, it had before it Judge Cardozo's opinion in the MacPherson case. That opinion was not binding and the federal court was free to disregard it. In fact, it was almost obliged, because of its own prior decision, to disregard the MacPherson opinion. But that is not what happened. The federal Circuit Court of Appeals, its personnel now somewhat changed, was persuaded by the MacPherson opinion and it overruled its own prior decisions. It quoted the language of Judge Cardozo, and then went on to explain why it was indulging in such an extraordinary reversal of ordinary judicial form. It said:

> We recognize the full force and effect of the doctrine of stare decisis, and the general rule that on a second appeal matters disposed of on the first appeal ordinarily will not be again considered. It is, like the rule of res adjudicata, not a mere rule of practice inherited from a more technical time than ours. It is a rule "of public policy and of private peace," and is to be cordially regarded and followed in all proper cases. [Citations] But the rule is not an inexorable one, and should not be adhered to in a case in which the court has committed an error which results in injustice, and at the same time lays down a principle of law for future guidance which is unsound and contrary to the interests of society. We are satisfied that the present case falls under the exception to which we have referred. We shall not consider at length the reasons which have satisfied us that a serious mistake was made in the first decision. The reasons may be found in the opinion in the Buick Case, to which we have already referred, and which render it unnecessary to traverse the ground anew. We cannot believe that the liability of a manufacturer of automobiles has any analogy to the liability of a manufacturer of "tables, chairs, pictures

or mirrors hung on walls." The analogy is rather that of a manufacturer of unwholesome food or of a poisonous drug. It is every bit as dangerous to put upon the market an automobile with rotten spokes as it is to send out to the trade rotten food-stuffs.[20]

So both Johnson and MacPherson finally triumphed. They did so because of ethical ideas, outside of existing legal rules, which were first entertained by two trial judges and two juries. Only later were those ideas accepted by appellate judges and thereby transformed in to a new legal rule.

The School Segregation Case

One more case will underline the extent to which changing ethical ideas decide questions of law and in the process determine rules for future cases. It is the famous decision by the Supreme Court of the United States in 1954 outlawing segregation in public schools. For at least half a century that Court and the country had been relying on the proposition that "separate but equal" facilities for Negro and white children were permissible. In abrogating that rule, the Supreme Court said:

> In approaching this problem, we cannot turn the clock back to 1868 when the Amendment was adopted, or even to 1896 when Plessy v. Ferguson was written. We must consider public education in the light of its full development and its present place in American life throughout the Nation. Only in this way can it be determined if segregation in public schools deprives these plaintiffs of the equal protection of the laws. . . .
> The effect of this separation on their educational opportunities was well stated by a finding in the Kansas case by a court which nevertheless felt compelled to rule against the Negro plaintiffs:
> > Segregation of white and colored children in public schools has a detrimental effect upon the colored children. The im-

pact is greater when it has the sanction of the law; for the policy of separating the races is usually interpreted as denoting the inferiority of the Negro group. A sense of inferiority affects the motivation of a child to learn. Segregation with the sanction of law, therefore, has a tendency to [retard] the educational and mental development of Negro children and to deprive them of some of the benefits they would receive in a racial[ly] integrated school system.

Whatever may have been the extent of psychological knowledge at the time of Plessy v. Ferguson, this finding is amply supported by modern authority. Any language in Plessy v. Ferguson contrary to this finding is rejected.

We conclude that in the field of public education the doctrine of "separate but equal" has no place. Separate educational facilities are inherently unequal.[21]

This is conscious law-making, akin to legislation except for the fact that it is done by a court rather than a legislature. It is in the tradition of the early English Court of Chancery where no pretense was made that the law had to remain static. Of less conscious law-making, in the tradition of the common-law courts of England where changes are seldom perceived until they have long been in effect, we shall speak in the next chapter.

The Tempo of Change

Overrulings of previous decisions, as in the School Segregation case, expose too nakedly for the peace of mind of some observers the law-making function of the courts. Those who prefer a neater separation of the powers of government point to the example of England where the courts leave changes in the law to Parliament, refusing to take upon themselves the task of overruling precedents even when convinced that the precedents are wrong or unsuited to present conditions.

But England has no written constitution. If it had one,

restricting even Parliament, and if such a constitution were as difficult to amend as our own, the English courts, forced into dealing with questions that are more clearly ones of policy than of law, might be tempted to adopt the American approach in its interpretation; otherwise an English constitution might be thoroughly ineffective.

American courts do not limit themselves to overruling precedents in constitutional interpretations. They function similarly in areas of statutory and judge-made law, correcting old errors and adapting the law to changed conditions and changing ideas. In these two areas the courts are on more questionable ground, for the rules with which they deal are not beyond legislative correction. Curiously enough, however, they seldom receive such sharp criticism for overrulings in these areas as they do in the area of constitutional law, where the justification for overruling outmoded precedents is demonstrably greater. Perhaps the reason for greater public concern with constitutional decisions is the fact that they deal with profound questions of public policy that affect vital interests and indeed the basic character of our society. Not to be overlooked either is the fact that constitutional decisions themselves are beyond legislative alteration; they require either constitutional amendment or a change of heart on the part of the court.

The problem is one of tempo rather than function. That courts can, do, and should make adjustments in the law is not seriously disputed. But how speedily should the changes be made? And when are existing rules so well established that legislative action or constitutional amendment rather than judicial decision is needed for their alteration? These are questions upon which men differ in specific situations even when they agree in the abstract upon the proper function of courts. Thus, Justice Frankfurter, voting with the majority in a recent case to apply a long established rule, said:

To be sure, it is never too late for this Court to correct a misconception in an occasional decision, even on a rare occasion to change a rule of law that may have long persisted but also have long been questioned and only fluctuatingly applied. To say that everybody on the Court has been wrong for 150 years and that that which has been deemed part of the bone and sinew of the law should now be extirpated is quite another thing. Decision-making is not a mechanical process, but neither is this Court an originating law-maker. The admonition of Mr. Justice Brandeis that we are not a third branch of the Legislature should never be disregarded.

Justice Black, dissenting and voting to abrogate the rule, said:

> Ordinarily it is sound policy to adhere to prior decisions but this practice has quite properly never been a blind, inflexible rule. Courts are not omniscient. Like every other human agency, they too can profit from trial and error, from experience and reflection. As others have demonstrated, the principle commonly referred to as *stare decisis* has never been thought to extend so far as to prevent the courts from correcting their own errors. Accordingly, this Court has time and time again from the very beginning reconsidered the merits of its earlier decisions even though they claimed great longevity and repeated reaffirmation. . . . Indeed, the Court has a special responsibility where questions of constitutional law are involved to review its decisions from time to time and where compelling reasons present themselves to refuse to follow erroneous precedents; otherwise its mistakes in interpreting the Constitution are extremely difficult to alleviate and needlessly so. [Citations] [22]

Judges are expected to act more like conductors of music than composers, more like actors than playwrights. Some freedom of interpretation is allowed them, but not without limitation. Leonard Bernstein is a composer as well as a conductor, but when he leads the New York Philharmonic in Beethoven's Fifth Symphony, he is expected to play Beethoven, not Bernstein. Orson Welles is a playwright as well as an actor and director, but when he plays or directs Hamlet, he is expected to do Shakespeare, not Welles. Judges are expected to observe similar distinctions, hard though they may be to define.

The Separation of Powers

Whether courts make law slowly or rapidly, the fact that they make it at all is hard to accept. We have been brought up to believe that only legislatures make law and courts do nothing more than apply the law.

Such a crude theory of the separation of powers obscures the nature of the work being done by judges and juries. By focusing attention on a single aspect of judicial activity, another aspect, more interesting and creative than the first, is thrown into shadow. This hidden aspect is concerned with the judicial quest for justice—the development of new solutions for new situations and the discarding of old solutions (even for old situations) that have proved unsatisfactory. This is truly a creative function of the courts, and it is either ignored in the extreme separation-of-powers doctrine or looked upon as an aberration, as if judges and juries were overstepping their boundaries by concerning themselves with justice rather than the strict application of law.

Furthermore, the belief that judges only apply preexisting rules tends to blunt, if not degrade, the creative function. Some lawyers and judges who have been brought up in this belief themselves seem to be only dimly aware of what they are doing, like masons who work on a cathedral but see only the stones in their hands. They are creating law—inevitably—but since they are not fully conscious of their role, they are apt to proceed blindly and ineptly, failing to exercise the wisdom they possess and to assume the responsibility which is theirs. As F. S. Cohen remarked:

> Judges want their conduct to be free not only from their own doubts, but also from the doubts of others. The judge is apt to feel that ethics is a risky affair, and that the less he has to

do with questions about which men have argued for many ages the less likely will people be to cast doubts upon the judgments he utters. The slot machine doctrine of the judge's function, which teaches that judgments emerge from judges as gum comes forth from a vending machine, implies that a judge's beliefs about ethics have nothing to do with his work on the bench. This doctrine offers much aid and comfort to judges in moments of social stress. There is no use in kicking at a slot machine. Complaints must be referred to the owners. Public protests against the things that judges do or say must be referred to the proper law making bodies of state or nation, or when these bodies refuse to take the blame, to the Founding Fathers, who, being dead, pay even less heed to public clamor than do living judges. Why, indeed, should any judge defend his judgments on grounds of ethics when it is so easy to take refuge from the shafts of moral protest, by hiding behind the doctrine of the slot machine? [23]

Law is not, never has been, and never can be a completely static and all-embracing body of rules. Rules enacted today are intended to apply tomorrow and the day after, not yesterday and the day before. They are made by people whose knowledge is limited to the past and present and who cannot foresee everything that the future will bring. No legislative body has yet been able to anticipate all the changes—technological, institutional, in the relations between men, in their attitudes—that will take place while the rules they make are still in effect. In the meantime, before new legislative action can be taken, problems arise requiring the attention of the courts and calling for decision.

In view of the constancy of change, some statutes as well as constitutional provisions are almost forthright in delegating legislative power to courts. They seem to lay down definite rules, but their language is such that the actual meaning remains to be spelled out by the courts in the course of deciding cases. Thus, the Sherman Antitrust Act outlaws contracts and combinations "in restraint of trade." But Congress does not say *which* contracts or combinations or even *which* general types of contracts or combinations are in restraint of trade; it leaves those problems to future determination. As courts gradually define the key terms and redefine them in applying them to specific situations courts are legislating, at least interstitially. After such laws have long been on the books and applied to conditions never anticipated when they were passed the statutes are not necessarily redrafted. On the contrary, if the courts have done a reasonably good job of reflecting community sentiment on the new problems presented, redrafting would be merely a duplication of work already done, changing the form of the law but leaving its substance untouched. Even if courts have done a poor job by prevailing community standards, corrective legislation may not be forthcoming because of inertia and politics. In the meantime justice must be done in individual cases—by judges and juries.

If we look at history, the legislative role of the courts is clearly demonstrated. The common law, which comprises by far the greater bulk of the total law in force in England and the United States, is nothing more or less than that which has been made by judges in the course of deciding cases. The origin of that body of law and the development of it, stretching back over centuries, is dramatic proof that courts do more than merely apply the law—they make it too, as a by-product of deciding cases.

Chapter / *Twelve*

Fitting the Facts to the Law

Sometimes the law of a case fits its facts comfortably, as in the Hauptmann and Webster trials. Sometimes the fit is poor. If so, a satisfactory result can be achieved in either of two ways. One is described in the preceding chapter: the process of stretching and twisting the law, as in *MacPherson v. Buick*, or even forthrightly altering it, as in the School Segregation case. The other is the process of manhandling the facts so as to make them fit the law.

How this happens can be seen most comfortably in historical perspective. Contemporary examples will follow after we become accustomed to the idea.

The Action of Ejectment

In about the year 1500 in the common-law courts of England a new type of lawsuit evolved, called *ejectment*. It enabled a tenant of land to recover it from anyone who was unlawfully depriving him of possession. By standards of the times, a great forward step had been taken. The tenant was not only given rights that he had not enjoyed before but also the advantage of the most advanced and rational procedure then known. Trial was by jury, rather than by ordeal, battle, or compurgation. Interminable delays which plagued some of the more ancient remedies were eliminated.

The new action was the subject of envy by owners of property who, like tenants, also needed help in acquiring possession when it was wrongfully withheld from them. The legal obstacle was that more ancient remedies were available to them. These were not considered adequate for two principal reasons: first, the mode of trial was either by battle or a very primitive version of trial by jury; second, the defendant could delay trial almost endlessly by a variety of legally sanctioned excuses. If he became sick, for example, he was entitled to an adjournment for a year and a day; or if he went on a crusade the trial might be adjourned the number of years necessary to await his return.

It is not surprising, therefore, that efforts were made to extend the new remedy of ejectment to owners of property. The first step in the process was for the owner to make a lease to a third person, who then entered upon the land and waited until he was thrown off by the adverse occupant. The lease was made not for ordinary real estate purposes but for purposes of litigation. Its only object was to lay the foundation for an action of ejectment in behalf of the owner. The tenant was a mere straw man.

There were obvious disadvantages to this scheme. The "tenant" might be beaten up in the process of being thrown off the land; or undue delay might occur before his presence was discovered. Hence, a second straw man was introduced into the act. His job was to eject the first straw man. Thus, the dispossession of a tenant was accomplished with no danger to life or limb and the conditions for bringing the desired lawsuit were met. The real defendant was notified of the suit and given an opportunity to defend by a polite letter, signed "Your loving friend."

Then it occurred to someone that the farce entailed

needless trouble and expense and that it might be eliminated if the strange goings on might be imagined instead of enacted. Accordingly, it became the practice to allege that a lease had been made (not true) to John Doe (an imaginary person) and that he had been ejected (not true) by Richard Roe (another imaginary person). The judges cooperated by not allowing the defendant to deny that the fictitious events had taken place.

Thus, over the course of about a century, the owner of property was given a remedy supposedly denied him by the very rule of law under which he sought it. The facts of countless cases had been tortured to fit the rule. Formally, the law remained unchanged, but its results were entirely different from those that might have been expected from its verbal formulation. The change was gradual and very likely imperceptible at the time it was being made. When in subsequent decades and centuries it had become clear what had happened, scholars spoke of the development as an admirable example of the growth of law through fiction.

Less euphemistic description might have been in terms of the perjury, manufacturing of evidence, and false judging involved. The manipulations might have been regarded as reprehensible, even criminal, but for their timing. Since they were in response to the "felt necessities of the time" (a phrase that Justice Oliver Wendell Holmes used in another context to describe legal growth), all was forgiven.

The Action of Trover

Other historic examples of the growth of the law through fictions abound. One more will suffice to make it clear that the development of ejectment was not an isolated aberration in legal thinking, but a not uncommon example of one of the ways in which our present substantive rules came into being. The ancient action of *trover* originally dealt with a very limited situation where the plaintiff had lost something (say, a purse) and the defendant had found it and refused to give it back. In that situation the plaintiff was entitled to recover damages equal to the value of the property. Gradually, over the course of time, the action came to have a much wider scope; it could be used whenever the defendant exercised unlawful dominion over property belonging to the plaintiff. He might have stolen it, or deliberately destroyed it, or, having borrowed it from the plaintiff, refused to return it, or "converted" it in any one of a dozen other ways; but the case against him was always phrased in the language of the ancient papers: he had "casually found" what the plaintiff had "casually lost." Thus in the nineteenth century a plaintiff might allege that he had "casually lost" and the defendant had "casually found" twenty black stallions or a warehouse full of furniture. He would do so with a straight face, and his claim would be soberly considered by an equally straight-faced judge. In other words, the facts of his case would be fitted into a legal pigeonhole stretched out of shape so completely that its original contours were all but forgotten.

Modern Fictions Respecting Corporations

Coming to more recent times, corporate litigation is a field in which the growth of law through fictions can still be observed in progress. Rules governing the jurisdiction of courts were formulated in an era when corporations were unknown, and litigation, generally speaking, involved only natural persons. As corporations came into being and gradually took over a major share of business activity, the problem arose as to how to deal with them in court. It was solved not so much frontally—through an explicit revision of the rules—as obliquely—through fictions that attributed human characteristics to corporations and pretended that they were natural persons. Thus, a corporation was considered "present" within any state where it was doing business, and, by reason of such business, to have "consented" (though only "impliedly") to be sued in the courts of that state. The language was animistic, seemingly primitive, but the thought process was highly sophisticated, and on a par with that encountered in the development of the actions of ejectment and trover. Again judges, without saying so, were refashioning the law to accommodate changing conditions.

In the federal courts, this process can be observed in amusing detail. Those courts possess only such powers as are allowed them by the United States Constitution. By that document they are given power to handle, along with certain other classes of cases, those which arise between "citizens" of different states. Corporations are not mentioned. In 1806, the Supreme Court was faced with the question of whether a corporation might qualify as a citizen under this provision. The answer first given was no—a corporation was not a human being but an artificial entity possessing neither "residence" or "citizenship." The Supreme Court, however, opened the door a little. It said that a corporation might be treated like a partnership, so that if all of its members—i.e., stockholders—were citizens of state A and if the other party was a citizen of state B, a federal court could assume jurisdiction. This helped a little but not much, because it didn't allow suit by or against a large corporation whose stockholders lived in several states.

The problem of the large corporation came before the Supreme Court a few decades later. The members of the Court, having by this time decided that corporations should be litigants in the federal courts under the diversity of citizenship clause, now introduced a presumption that all of a corporation's stockholders resided in the state of its incorporation. This was patently false but it did the job. To insure that the truth could not be inquired into, the Court made the presumption conclusive. Thenceforth, no one was allowed to claim or prove, for the purpose of defeating the jurisdiction of a federal court, that the stockholders of a corporate litigant were citizens of different states.

Bunn, a student of the federal courts, after describing the development outlined above, goes on to say:

This remains still the ground of jurisdiction over corporations. The jurisdiction does not rest on the corporation being a citizen, for it is not, but on the presumption, which is a pure fiction, but which cannot be disputed or traversed, that all its stockholders are citizens of the particular State where the corporation was organized. So for the purpose of jurisdiction, a corporation is treated as if it were a citizen of the State where it is incorporated.

The story didn't end there, however. Congress, which was just as much bound by the Constitution as the Supreme Court, but which was so pleased by the extension of federal jurisdiction over ordinary corporations that it wanted to extend it still further over national banks as well, twisted a few more facts to bring these organizations under the governing constitutional rule. Bunn describes this development as follows:

> The Supreme Court having created this frank fiction for the purpose of giving jurisdiction, Congress has added another. National Banks (which of course are corporations under Federal law) are for the purposes of private actions "deemed citizens of the States in which they are respectively located." (28 U.S.C.A. Section 1348). This fiction also cannot be contradicted. So that adding the two together if an action for $3,001 were brought for instance by the National City Bank of New York (which is a corporation under federal law with headquarters in New York), against the General Motors Corporation (which is incorporated under the laws of Delaware), in a United States District Court on any cause of action, the Court would have jurisdiction on the theory that the Bank is a citizen of New York (which it is not) and that all the stockholders of General Motors are citizens of Delaware (which they certainly are not). This is one of the things that causes scientists and other literal-minded people to say that lawyers believe in magic. We may not admit that fully, but we shall indeed have to confess that there is nothing unlawyerlike in using fictions to accomplish a result.[24]

Even then the manufacture of fictions did not cease. After the Second World War the dockets of the federal courts became overcrowded, in part because of heavy corporate litigation. There were too many suits for the judges to handle between corporations incorporated in one state but doing business in another and the citizens of the latter states. In 1958, Congress did an about face; it decided to curtail rather than extend the jurisdiction of federal courts over such suits and thus force them back into state courts. It did so by another fiction, whereby a corporation would be deemed a citizen not only of the state where it was incorporated but also of the state where it had its principal place of business.[25] Thereafter, a corporation incorporated in Delaware but having its principal place of business in New York could no longer sue a New York citizen or be sued by him in a federal court, because the parties were no longer citizens of different states.

This, then, is still another fiction, of very recent origin, superimposed on the others already described and, like them, designed to accomplish results considered desirable. Meanwhile, during the entire period of about 150 years of development of federal jurisdiction over corporations, the words of the constitutional provision on jurisdiction remained unaltered. The practical effect of the rule had been radically altered, but not its text. Facts had been twisted and given different names to accommodate them under the old rule to achieve a result that might equally well and much more forthrightly have been accomplished by a change in the rule itself.

Modern Divorce Litigation

Not all fictions deal only with technical problems like jurisdiction. Some operate in areas where deep questions of morals and social policy are involved. Such are the fictions that are found today in divorce cases and negligence cases, about to be discussed.

In New York, where the sole ground of divorce is adultery, a girl in black lingerie is found so often in hotel rooms with the husbands of other ladies that she has become almost as much a creature of fiction as John Doe or Richard Roe who figured so prominently in the ancient action of ejectment. Judge Morris Ploscowe indicates her role as follows:

To prove a case of actual adultery practically involves catching two people in the middle of a sexual act. If this were the standard insisted upon by courts, there would be few divorces for adultery. Courts, however, have had to be satisfied with a great deal less proof of adultery than catching a couple *in flagrante delicto*. They have been content with the appearance rather than the reality of adultery. Facts must be proved from which adultery can be inferred as a necessary conclusion. It is a necessary conclusion according to Judge Gaynor, that when a man and a woman not his wife retire to a bedroom of a hotel "it is presumed he saith not a pater noster."

Miller v. Miller is a typical hotel room case and illustrates the kind of evidence which results in thousands of people being divorced in New York every year. The husband in that case met a woman on a street corner, took her to a near-by hotel, and registered as man and wife. A short time later, the brother of the wife and a private detective went to this room, knocked on the door, announced that a bellboy wished to enter and gained admittance. The defendant had his coat, vest, collar and tie off and was in his shirt sleeves. The woman in the room had her shoes and dress off. The woman was not Mrs. Miller. There was a bottle of whisky and also a glass on the table.

The appellate court reversed a decision of the trial court which refused to grant a divorce for adultery on this evidence, stating in the course of its opinion

The allegations of the complaint (that the defendant committed adultery with an unknown woman) were established if the evidence in this case was true. There is nothing to indicate that it was untrue or that the trial justice dismissed the complaint because of his belief that the testimony was untrue. He placed the dismissal on the ground that the acts were as consistent with innocence as guilt. *Such a conclusion (innocence) is not consistent with* the acts of these parties.

New York courts have laid themselves wide open to perjury and collusion because of this practice of being satisfied with the appearance of adultery as a basis for granting a divorce. In fact, there is a strong probability that most New York divorces are collusive and perjurious.

A short time ago, a twenty-year-old woman, wife of a building superintendent and mother of three small children, complained to a newspaper reporter about the small fees she was getting serving as a professional co-respondent in divorce cases. She was the perennial unknown woman, not the wife of the defendant, with whom the defendant in the divorce case was found, in various stages of undress or in various compromising positions. Investigations of her story brought to light a genuine divorce mill which offered two kinds of services: (1) The setup job—a raid at a hotel room occupied by the co-operative husband and the unknown woman, and (2) The testimony job—which merely involved testimony about such a raid which never occurred, but which was conjured up out of thin air in the corridors of the courthouse, before the divorce case was called for a hearing.

In one of the latter types of cases, the district attorney discovered that the husband was actually in California at the time the testimony placed him in New York, in a hotel room, enjoying the favors of an unknown woman.

The grand jury investigation resulting from the above disclosures reviewed six hundred divorce cases and examined fifteen hundred witnesses. At the conclusion of its inquiry, it declared, "The manner in which uncontested matrimonial actions are conducted encourages laxity and other evils. . . . The investigation confirmed what had long been suspected: widespread fraud, perjury, collusion and connivance pervade matrimonial actions of every type. . . . The present practices exude a stench and perpetuate a scandal involving the courts and the community."

There is nothing new about the facts disclosed by the grand jury investigation. In the mid-thirties an analysis was made of a large number of records in divorce cases to determine the state of undress of the erring defendant and the co-respondent, when the witnesses for the aggrieved mate burst in upon them. The author of this analysis noted the uniformly surprising state of undress of the sinning parties and commented that people don't usually open a door to admit a stranger unless they are more suitably clothed. In 1936, Justice Bonynge of the New York Supreme Court commented on the judicial naivete which compelled the acceptance of collusive and false stories in divorce cases.

Has not my good brother overlooked the fact that a certain amount of naïvete is an essential adjunct to the judicial office? Does not the Supreme Court grind out thousands of divorces annually upon the stereotyped sin of the same big blonde attired in the same black silk pajamas? Is not access to the chamber of love quite uniformly obtained by announcing that it is a maid bringing towels or a messenger boy with an urgent telegram?

Occasionally a brave judge strikes out against a system that compels him to approve fraud, collusion and connivance as a means of obtaining a divorce in New York. But he usually finds that his moral indignation breaks against the rock of appellate court immobility. For example, Justice Henry Clay Greenberg overruled the reports of official referees recommending divorces in several cases. In one case a witness bearing the same name as the man seeking the divorce testified that the man's wife had a room in his house and that on a certain morning around 5 o'clock he "had to walk into her room and found her and her boyfriend in bed together . . . they were undressed." The judge wondered whether the witness was related to the husband; he wondered why he had to walk into her room at five in the morning without knocking and for no obvious reason. "His entire testimony reeks with grave suspicion and indicates strongly that the facts were manufactured to suit the plaintiff's objective," Justice Greenberg stated.

Less than a week later, he overruled the referee in another case in which the woman sought a divorce. Her mother was both the process server and the sole witness to the alleged act of adultery. Again Justice Greenberg wondered why the woman came to be at the particular address on the particular date; why the husband apparently showed no surprise when his mother-in-law discovered him with a woman not his wife; how the witness gained access to the apartment and why no attempt to eject her was made. "The record" he said, "is silent on these matters and this very silence is eloquent testimony that the action was not conceived in honesty." Remarking that the situation was intolerable, Justice Greenberg concluded, "The court is prepared to strike the first blow and to attempt to put an end to this monstrous sham where the forms are adhered to and where the structure is rooted in hypocrisy, connivance and deception."

The appellate court reversed Justice Greenberg's judgment and insisted without stating any reasons that the original decision of the referee must stand. Thus, this one-man attempt at reform of New York's collusive divorce procedures was stopped in its tracks. The New York courts continue to grind out day after day their fifteen to twenty uncontested divorces in precisely the same fashion which proved grist for the divorce mill uncovered by the Grand Jury.[26]

Some New York lawyers are righteously shocked by the thought of manufacturing evidence, but have no qualms about advising their divorce clients to go to Reno, Nevada. They know as well as the lawyers and judges of Nevada that according to the law there divorces can be granted only to "bona fide" residents of the state. They know too, or at least suspect, that their clients have no intention of moving permanently to Nevada. Yet the advice is still given; and some of the clients probably even purchase round-trip tickets. After they arrive in Nevada and put in their minimum period of six weeks' residence, they still have to establish grounds for a divorce. This frequently involves additional perjury beyond the question of domicile, for mere incompatibility with one's spouse is not legally enough. "Extreme cruelty" is, however; and that is the ground for divorce most often and conveniently chosen regardless of the actual relations between the parties. So a divorce is granted, and the parties live more or less happily ever afterward.

Can it be that, despite all divorce laws to the contrary,

the true bases for divorce throughout the United States are (1) consent and (2) incompatibility? And that the only conditions for divorce are not legal but economic and temperamental, namely, that the person seeking the divorce have enough money and patience to suffer through whatever ritualistic formalities are prescribed? If so, it is because facts are being twisted to conform to law. The divorce statutes stand unchanged.

But divorce litigation, it may be argued, is not typical because it is so often collusive. With both sides seeking the same result, the use of fictions is at least understandable, if not laudable.

Auto Accident Litigation

If further proof is needed of the growth of modern law through fictions, it can be found in the field of auto accident cases. These are ordinarily contested with vigor, and along with divorce cases, they account for the great bulk of the civil business of our major courts today.

In the last chapter we observed how juries are recasting the law of contributory negligence into the vastly different law of comparative negligence. This could not occur without a bit of judicious perjury about the conduct of plaintiffs in such cases. As might be expected, such chicanery is not openly acknowledged by plaintiffs, their lawyers, jurors, or judges. But that it exists on a large scale is illustrated by the following story. A judge, crossing a street against a traffic light, was admonished by his companions to be more careful. "You of all people," said one of his friends, "should know better." "On the contrary," replied the judge. "I am convinced that this is the only safe way to cross a street. In twenty years of experience trying personal injury cases, I have never known a plaintiff to be injured while crossing against a light, but I have known many who were injured while crossing when the light was in their favor."

Thus again facts are molded to fit existing rules of law in order to achieve results thought to be desirable. While the process is exactly the reverse of that involved in *MacPherson v. Buick* and the School Segregation case described in the preceding chapter the net result is the same. Indeed, so far as juries are concerned, even the processes are scarcely distinguishable. Being under no compulsion to write opinions or otherwise express the reasons for their decisions, jurors need not bother their heads about whether they are molding facts to fit law or law to fit facts. They are free to indulge in a general *gestalt*. The important thing to them is the result, the doing of justice in the individual case according to their own lights. Regardless of which process is involved the ultimate determinants of decision are the same, namely, ethical ideas not embodied in existing rules of law, which the jurors bring with them when they first walk into the courtroom.

Summary

The realization that facts are sometimes twisted to fit law and that law is sometimes twisted to fit facts is no cause for dismay. The processes are inevitable in changing civilization. New inventions and discoveries transform society, and men and their ideas continue to develop. Unless law is to be nothing more than a dead hand from the past, it must change too. Legislation has never yet been equal to the task of adequate legal development, for such legislation involves a degree of foresight not yet vouchsafed to mortals. Hence a large share of responsibility falls upon those charged with making decisions in individual cases. Were it not for the fact of change most of the work of judges could be entrusted to file clerks. The only intellectual effort would be finding the appropriate rules—a matter of almost mechanical research. Indeed, the matter of making legal decisions could even be entrusted to IBM machines. After the facts had been ascertained (though how this could be done by machines is beyond imagination), all that would be necessary would be to insert a card bearing the facts into a machine where previous decisions were catalogued and filed, press a button, and the judgment would tumble out. Happily for the self-respect and economic security of the legal profession as well as the well being of society in general, the process is not quite so simple.

If, however, the task of adapting law to a changing society seems too uncertain and difficult, it may be comforting to adopt the attitude toward law described by Sir Henry Maine about a century ago:

We in England are well accustomed to the extension, modification, and improvement of law by a machinery which, in theory, is incapable of altering one jot or one line of existing jurisprudence. The process by which this virtual legislation is effected is not so much insensible as unacknowledged. With respect to that great portion of our legal system which is enshrined in cases and recorded in law reports, we habitually employ a double language, and entertain, as it would appear, a double and inconsistent set of ideas. When a group of facts comes before an English Court for adjudication, the whole course of the discussion between the judge and the advocates assumes that no question is, or can be, raised which will call for the application of any principles but old ones, or of any distinctions but such as have long since been allowed. It is taken absolutely for granted that there is somewhere a rule of known law which will cover the facts of the dispute now litigated, and that, if such a rule be not discovered, it is only that the necessary patience, knowledge, or acumen is not forthcoming to detect it. Yet the moment the judgment had been rendered and reported, we slide unconsciously or unavowedly into a new language and a new train of thought. We now admit that the new decision has modified the law. The rules applicable have, to use the very inaccurate expression sometimes employed, become more elastic. In fact they have been changed. A clear addition has been made to the precedents, and the canon of law elicited by comparing the precedents is not the same with that which would have been obtained if the series of cases had been curtailed by a single example. The fact that the old rule has been repealed, and that a new one has replaced it, eludes us, because we are not in the habit of throwing into precise language the legal formulas which we derive from the precedents, so that a change in their tenor is not easily detected unless it is violent and glaring. . . .

We do not admit that our tribunals legislate; we imply that they have never legislated; and yet we maintain that the rules of the English common law, with some assistance from the Court of Chancery and from Parliament, are coextensive with the complicated interests of modern society.[27]

"A government of laws, not of men," is a comforting ideal, but not a very realistic one. Men must interpret and apply laws in the context of a changing society. Not only are things and conditions changing constantly but also people's attitudes toward them and toward each other. There is continuity, of course, between one generation and the next, in law as well as in other areas, but there is also change. If even history has to be rewritten for each generation, and if, as Heraclitus said, no man can step into the same stream twice, what reason is there to suppose that law is not also in need of and in the process of continual revision?

Justice Holmes once said that "general principles do not decide concrete cases."

People do.

Notes

1 Arthur T. Vanderbilt, "The Municipal Court," 10 *Rutgers L. Rev.* 650 (1956).

2 304 U.S. 64 (1938).

3 *Gideon v. Wainwright,* 372 U.S. 335 (1963). (This case also traces developments in earlier cases.)

4 *Griffin v. Illinois,* 351 U.S. 12 (1956).

5 *Thompson v. City of Louisville,* 362 U.S. 199 (1960).

6 1 Cranch 137 (1803).

7 *Baker v. Carr,* 369 U.S. 186 (1962).

8 *Engel v. Vitali,* 370 U.S. 421 (1962).

9 *Brown v. Board of Education,* 347 U.S. 483 (1954).

10 Frederic W. Maitland, *The Forms of Action at Common Law* (Cambridge, England: Cambridge University Press, 1936), pp. 15-16. Reprinted by permission of the publisher.

11 George Bemis, *Report of the Case of John W. Webster* (Boston: C. C. Little and James Brown, 1850), pp. 564-567.

12   Martin M. Frank, *Diary of a D.A.* (New York: Holt, Rinehart and Winston, Inc., 1960), p. 182.

13   *Berry v. Chaplin*, 169 P. 2d 442 (1946).

14   Sidney B. Schatkin, "The Scandal of Our Paternity Courts," 76 *Readers Digest* 71 (May 1960).

15   *Bemis, op. cit.* pp. 456-457.

16   A. P. Herbert, *Misleading Cases in the Common Law* (London: Methuen & Co., Ltd., 1927), p. 10.

17   Joseph N. Ulman, *A Judge Takes the Stand* (New York: Alfred A. Knopf, Inc., 1932), pp. 30-32. Reprinted by permission of the publisher.

18   *Cadillac Motor Co. v. Johnson*, 221 Fed. 801 (1915). At the time this case was decided, federal courts applied their own ideas of substantive law. Since the decision in *Erie Railroad v. Tompkins*, 304 U.S. 64 (1938), federal courts, in a situation like that presented in the Cadillac case, are required to apply state law.

19   *MacPherson v. Buick Motor Co.*, 217 N.Y. 382 (1916).

20   *Johnson v. Cadillac Motor Car Co.*, 261 Fed. 878 (1919).

21   *Brown v. Board of Education*, 347 U.S. 483 (1954).

22   Both quotations are from *Green v. United States*, 356 U.S. 165 (1958).

23   Cohen and Cohen, *Readings in Jurisprudence and Legal Philosophy* (Englewood Cliffs, N.J.: Prentice-Hall, Inc., 1951), p. 647.

24   Both quotations are from Charles Bunn, *Jurisdiction and Practice of the Courts of the United States* (St. Paul, Minn.: West Publishing Company, Fifth ed., 1949) pp. 45-46. At the time the book was written, the jurisdictional amount for diversity of citizenship cases was $3000. It has now been raised to $10,000. 28 U.S. Code, Sec. 1332.

25   For the current provision, see 28 U.S. Code, Sec. 1332 (c).

26   Morris Ploscowe, *The Truth About Divorce* (New

York: Hawthorn Books, Inc., 1955), pp. 99-102. Reprinted by permission of the publisher.

27 Henry Maine, *Ancient Law* (New York: Charles Scribner & Sons, First American ed., 1864), pp. 29-31.

Glossary

of Terms

ALLEGATION A statement in a pleading of a party's claim or defense.

APPELLANT The person who takes an appeal, seeking reversal or modification of a trial court decision.

APPELLEE The person against whom an appeal is taken. The party, in other words, who is trying to sustain a trial court decision.

ARRAIGNMENT The step in a criminal case where the accusation is read aloud to the defendant, and he is asked to plead guilty or not guilty.

BAIL The deposit of money or the posting of a bond to ensure that a person accused of crime will appear at his trial. It allows the defendant to be at liberty (out of jail) until the time of trial.

BRIEF A written argument submitted to a court, usually only in connection with cases on appeal.

CERTIORARI The process whereby the Supreme Court of the United States decides which cases it wishes to review among those offered to it.

CITATIONS References to legal authorities or decided cases.

COMMON LAW In its most frequently used sense, the law made by judges in the course of deciding cases; in a more technical sense, the law developed in certain English courts.

CONCURRENT JURISDICTION   Jurisdiction over a given type of case that is shared by two or more courts.

CONCURRING OPINION   A statement by an appellate court judge of why he agrees with the result reached by a majority of his colleagues and why he disagrees with their reasoning.

CONTINGENT FEE   One where the lawyer's compensation depends upon his achieving a successful result for his client.

DEFAULT JUDGMENT   Judgment entered in a civil case where the defendant does not contest the claim asserted against him. Thus, uncontested, the case is won by the plaintiff.

DIRECTED VERDICT   A determination by the judge that the facts of a case are so clear that he does not need to submit the case to jury.

DISSENTING OPINION   A statement by an appellate court judge of the reasons why he disagrees with the decision reached by a majority of his colleagues.

DISTRICT COURT   In the federal system, the only type of trial court that exists; in state systems, also a trial court, with jurisdiction varying from state to state.

DOCKET   The record of the list of cases waiting to be tried.

EXCLUSIVE JURISDICTION   The power given to one court, as against all others, to handle a given type of case.

EXTRADITION   The process by which a person, who is alleged to have committed a crime in a certain place and then to have fled, is brought back to the place of the crime for trial.

FELONY   A very serious crime generally punishable by death or imprisonment.

GARNISHEE   The process whereby a person holding money belonging to another, such as an employer or a bank, can be required to pay it over directly to that person's creditor.

GRAND JURY   A body of citizens who hear evidence of

crimes and decide whether and whom to prosecute.

INDICTMENT   A form of accusation of crime made by a grand jury.

INFORMATION   A form of accusation of crime made by a district attorney rather than a grand jury.

JUDGMENT   The document embodying the final result of a trial.

JURISDICTION   The power or authority of a court to deal with a given case.

LITIGANT   One who is involved in a lawsuit as a party. Both the plaintiff and the defendant in a civil action are litigants.

MAGISTRATE   The judge of an inferior court who tries minor cases, civil and criminal and who conducts preliminary hearings in serious criminal cases.

MAJORITY OPINION   The statement written by one appellate judge on behalf of a majority of his colleagues setting forth the conclusion of the court and the reasons therefor.

MISDEMEANOR   A crime whose seriousness is regarded as less than that of a felony but greater than that of an offense.

MUNICIPAL COURT   A court empowered to try minor cases. The jurisdiction of such a court varies from state to state and from city to city within a state.

OFFENSE   A minor crime carrying a light penalty.

PETITION   A written request to a court for action upon a stated matter.

PETIT JURY   A jury empaneled to try criminal or civil cases.

PLEA   The original answer given by the defendant to the accusation against him—usually *guilty* or *not guilty*.

PRECEDENT   A prior decision or authority that guides the court in deciding a case currently before it.

PRELIMINARY HEARING   An early stage of a criminal case designed to see whether there is sufficient evidence to justify holding the accused for trial.

PROBATE COURT A court that handles the distribution of the estate of a decedent.

PROCEDURAL LAW That part of the law that controls the mechanics of bringing conducting and deciding a lawsuit.

PROSECUTION The bringing of a criminal proceeding or the authority conducting such a proceeding.

RESPONDENT The appellee or person who defends an appeal. He is trying to sustain the result reached in the court below.

SUBSTANTIVE LAW That part of law that defines rights and duties.

SUMMARY JUDGMENT The disposition of a civil case without trial on the basis that the facts are so clear that reasonable men could not differ about them.

SUMMONS The initial paper served upon the defendant to commence a civil action.

TORT A civil wrong done by one person to another which the courts recognize as justifying an award of damages or other sanction.

TRIBUNAL A court or administrative agency that decides questions of law or fact or both.

VENUE The location where a trial is to be held.

WAIVER The voluntary relinquishment of a right.

WARRANT A court order authorizing the arrest of a person or the search or seizure of property belonging to him.

Bibliography

Bedford, Sybille. *The Faces of Justice.* New York: Simon and Schuster, Inc., 1961. (How ordinary cases are handled in England, Germany, Austria, Switzerland, and France.)

Bowen, Catherine D. *Yankee from Olympus.* Boston: Little, Brown & Company, 1944. (An excellent biography of Justice Oliver Wendell Holmes, Jr.)

Cahn, Edmond. *The Moral Decision.* Bloomington: Indiana University Press, 1956. (A study of law and ethics in the light of concrete cases.)

Cardozo, Benjamin N. *The Nature of the Judicial Process.* New Haven, Conn.: Yale University Press, 1921. (A distinguished judge explains how an appellate court reaches its decisions.)

Cozzens, James G. *The Just and the Unjust.* New York: Harcourt, Brace & World, Inc., 1942. (An excellent novel on the day-to-day life of a lawyer.)

Dickens, Charles. *Pickwick Papers.* First published in 1837, but now available in many editions. (Hilarious account of a breach of promise of marriage suit, providing deep insight into English law during the early nineteenth century.)

Dostoevsky, Feodor. *Crime and Punishment.* First published in 1866, but now available in many editions. (Classic brooding novel about the disintegration of an intellectual who considered himself above the law and ordinary standards of morality.)

203

Frank, Jerome. *Law and the Modern Mind*. New York: Coward-McCann, Inc., 1949. (A study of the relationship of law and psychology by an iconoclastic practitioner, judge, and law teacher.)

Herbert, Alan P. *Misleading Cases in the Common Law*. London: Methuen & Co., Ltd., Fourth ed., 1928; New York: G. P. Putnam's Sons, 1930. (Wonderfully funny stories about the legal mind at work.)

Holmes, Oliver Wendell. *The Common Law*. Cambridge, Mass.: Harvard University Press, 1963. (A very difficult but rewarding classic that analyzes the growth of law through judicial decisions.)

Hurst, James W. *The Growth of American Law*. Boston: Little, Brown & Company, 1950. (An evaluation of the sources of legal growth—legislative, constitutional, executive, and professional as well as judicial.)

Jackson, R. M. *The Machinery of Justice in England*. Cambridge, England: University Press, Third ed., 1960. (The best short description of English law and legal institutions today.)

Jackson, Robert H. *The Supreme Court*. Cambridge, Mass.: Harvard University Press, 1955. (One of its justices explains the role of the Supreme Court in the American system of government.)

Mayers, Lewis. *The American Legal System*. New York: Harper & Row, Publishers, Rev. ed., 1964. (A comprehensive text on the machinery of justice in the United States.)

Parker, James R. *Attorneys at Law*. Garden City, N. Y.: Doubleday & Company, Inc., 1941. (Stories, which originally appeared in the *New Yorker* magazine, about the day-to-day activities in a Wall Street law firm.)

Pound, Roscoe. *The Spirit of the Common Law*. Boston: Marshall Jones Co., 1921. (An exposition by a leading legal philosopher of the nature of judge-made law.)

Stone, Irving. *Clarence Darrow for the Defense*. New York: Doubleday & Company, Inc., 1948. (The career of a very famous trial lawyer.)

Train, Arthur C. *Yankee Lawyer*. New York: Charles Scribner's Sons, 1943. (A fictional autobiography of a fictional lawyer, much beloved for his wily stratagems in good causes.)

Ullman, Joseph N. *A Judge Takes the Stand*. New York: Alfred A. Knopf, Inc., 1933. (Reflective, thoughtful memoirs by a trial judge, explaining his functions and his relationships to the jury, the litigants, the lawyers, and the appellate courts.)

Vanderbilt, Arthur T. *The Challenge of Law Reform*. Princeton, N. J.: Princeton University Press, 1955. (An exposition of some of the problems facing the courts and of solutions for them. Written by a man who was one of the leading law reformers of modern times as well as a noted judge, legal educator, and practicing lawyer.)

Waller, George. *Kidnap*. New York: The Dial Press, Inc., 1961. (An account, written long after the event, of one of America's most famous criminal trials—that of Bruno Hauptmann for the kidnapping and murder of the Lindbergh baby.)

Williams, Edward Bennett. *One Man's Freedom*. New York: Atheneum Publishers, 1962. (A largely autobiographical account by a well-known criminal lawyer of the problems involved in the representation of unpopular causes and clients.)

Index

Adhesion, 64-65

Administrative Office of the United States Courts, 109

Administrative tribunals, 103-105

Annulment, 82

Answer, 74

Appeals, 87-98

Appearance, 83-84

Appellant, 90

Appellate courts, 6-7, 22-23

Appellee, 91

Arraignment, 33-34, 46

Arrest, 28, 39

Auto accident litigation, 64-79, 159-163, 191-192

Bail, 43-44

Baker v. Carr, 101-102

Beck case, 149

Bill collection cases, 58-63

Briefs, 91

Bunn, Charles, 184-185

Burden of proof, 52, 77

Campbell case, 149-150

Cardozo, Benjamin N., 166

Certiorari, 98

Challenges, for cause, 49

peremptory, 49

Chaplin paternity case, 151-154

Charge to jury, 52

Choice of law, 18-19

Circumstantial evidence, 131, 136-154

Civil liability, 64-66

Cohen, F. S., 177-178

Collusion in divorce actions, 84

Common law, 8-11, 179

Comparative negligence, 191

Complaint, 71

Conciliation in divorce cases, 80-81

Concurring opinions, 93

Congress, legislative power of, 8

Consistency as factor in credibility, 128

Constitution of the United

States, due process clause, 14

full faith and credit clause, 14

supremacy clause, 12

Contingent fees, 67

Contradiction as factor in credibility, 132

Contributory negligence, 161-163, 191-192

Corporations, federal jurisdiction, 183-186

Corroboration as factor in credibility, 132

Counsel, right to, 34

Counsel for indigents, 47, 91

Counterclaim, 74-75

Court administration, 109

Court organization, 108-109

Court-packing plan, 109

Courts, appellate, 6-7
    federal, 21-25
    state, 3-7
    trial, 3-6

Credibility, 122-135

Crimes, federal and state, 15-16

Cross-examination, 35, 50, 63

Default judgment, 72, 84

Demeanor as factor in credibility, 134

Denials in answer, 74

Deterrence as goal of criminal law, 31, 36

Direct evidence, 149

Directed verdict, 164-165

of acquittal, 51
    civil cases, 77

Discovery, 75-76

Dissenting opinions, 93

District attorney, 40-41

District courts of United States, 21-22

Divorce litigation, 80-86, 186-191

Ejectment, 180-182

England, practice on appeals, 91-94

Erie Railroad v. Tompkins, 19

Ethical and legal concepts, 165-174

Euthanasia case, 158

Execution of judgment, 61, 78-79

Extradition, 41-42

Extraordinary remedies, 106

Federal courts, 21-25

Federal jurisdiction, 69
    diversity of citizenship, 17-18
    federal questions, 16-17

Federal questions, jurisdiction of Supreme Court, 96

Fees, 67

Felony, 38

Fictions and legal growth, 180-186

Fines, 31-32

Forma pauperis appeals, 90

Full faith and credit, 14, 79, 86

Garnishment, 62
Grand jury, 39, 45
Green v. United States, 175-
176
Guilty plea, 32-33

Habeas corpus, 105
Hauptmann case, 121-135
Holmes, Oliver W., Jr., 166,
182

Impeachment of judges, 108
Indeterminate sentence, 55
Indictment, 28, 45
Indigents, counsel for, 47, 91
Inferences, 136-154
Inferior courts, 4-5
Information, 28, 45
Injunction, 66, 106
Instructions to jury, 52, 78,
156-157
Interest as factor in credi-
bility, 35, 125
Intermediate appellate courts,
95

Judges, appointment, 107
election, 107
retirement, 111
salaries, 111
selection, 107, 110
tenure, 107, 111
Judgment, 61, 78
Judicial Conference of United
States, 109
Judicial law-making, 173-179
Judicial review, administrative
tribunals, 103

Constitutionality of statutes,
98-100
executive action, 102
Jurisdiction, 86
civil cases, 13-14, 29
concurrent, 21
criminal cases, 11-13, 29-30
exclusive, 21
federal, 14-20, 69
Jury, in divorce actions, 85
right to trial by, 33, 48-49,
63, 76
Justice of the peace, 4-5, 30
Juvenile court proceedings, 5-
6

Legal aid, 48
Legislative power, allocation
between nation and states,
7-8
Lindbergh case, 121-135

*MacPherson v. Buick Motor
Co.,* 167-173
Magistrate, 43
Maine, Sir Henry, 193-194
Maitland, F. W., 119-120
Mandamus, 106
Marbury v. Madison, 100
Misdemeanor, 38
Missouri plan of judicial selec-
tion, 110
Motion to dismiss, 73
Motion to strike, 74
Municipal court, 28-30
New trial, 53, 77

Nonresident motorist statute, 69
Not guilty plea, 33-35

Offense, 38
Opening statements, 49
Opinions, 92
Oral argument on appeal, 91
Overruling precedents, 174-179

Parkman murder, 136-148
Parole, 56
Paternity cases, 151-154
Personal injury litigation, 64-79
Plea, guilty, 32-33, 45-46
  not guilty, 33-35
Pleading, oral and written, 62, 71, 74
Ploscowe, Morris, 187-190
Police, role of, 27, 34, 40-41
Postconviction proceedings, 56-57
Precedent, 8-9, 93, 165-166
Prejudicial error, 89
Preliminary hearing, 43-44
Presentence investigation, 54
Presumption of innocence, 52, 140
Pretrial conference, 76
Prior inconsistent statement, 128
Privilege against self-incrimination, 35, 44, 50-51
Probability as gauge of credibility, 129-131

Procedural rule-making power, 112
Procedure, laws of forum applied, 70
Prohibition, 106
Public-defender systems, 48
Publicity and fair trial, 152
Punishment, 36-39

Quo warranto, 106

Reapportionment case, 101-102
Record on appeal, 90
Recross-examination, 50
Redirect examination, 50
Reformation as goal of criminal law, 31, 36
Remedies, 66
Removal of cases from state to federal court, 19-20
Reply, 75
Res judicata, 79
Respondent, 91
Robbery prosecution, 38-58

Sacco-Vanzetti case, 153
School prayer case, 102
School segregation case, 173
Scottsboro case, 153
Selection of judges, 110
Sentencing, 36-37, 54
  appellate review, 55, 89
  institutes, 55
Separation of powers, 177-179
Settlement, 67

Soblen spy case, 105
Special verdict, 163-164
Stare decisis, 174-179
State court structure, 3-7
Statute of limitations, 68
Summary judgment, 75
Summons, 59, 68, 71
Supreme Court of the United
    States, 7, 14-15, 22-23
    43, 95

Tenure of judges, 107

Traffic offenses, 26-37
Trial, 33-35
Trial courts, 3-6
Trial *de novo*, 88
Trover, 182-183

Venue, 59
Verdict, special, 163-164
    unanimity, 77-78
Violations bureaus, 31-32

Webster case, 136-148

Sohlen spy case, 105
Special verdict, 163-164
State dockets, 176-179
State court structure, 5-7
Statute of limitations, 66
Summary judgment, 75
Suppress, 19, 63, 71
Supreme Court of the United
States, 7, 14-15, 22-37
43, 95

Tenure of judges, 107

Traffic offenses, 26-37
Trial, 54-55
Trial courts, 5-6
Trial de novo, 88
Traver, 152-153

Venue, 59
Verdict, special, 163-164
unanimity, 77-78
Violations bureaus, 31-32

Webster case, 135-148